Contents

On the Mountainside

*M*ore than fourteen centuries before Jesus was born in Bethlehem, the children of Israel gathered in the fair vale of Shechem, and from the mountains on either side the voices of the priests were heard proclaiming the blessings and the curses—"the blessing, if you obey the commandments of the Lord your God"; "the curse, if you do not obey" (Deuteronomy 11:27, 28). And thus the mountain from which the words of benediction were spoken came to be known as the mount of blessing.

But no longer is Gerizim known as the mount of the Beatitudes; it is that unnamed mountain beside the Lake of Gennesaret where Jesus spoke the words of blessing to His disciples and the multitude.

Let us in imagination go back to that scene, and, as we sit with the disciples on the mountainside, enter into the thoughts and feelings that filled their hearts. Understanding what the words of Jesus meant to those who heard them, we may discern in them a new vividness and beauty, and may also gather for ourselves their deeper lessons.

When the Savior began His ministry, the popular conception of the Messiah and His work was such as wholly unfitted the people to receive Him. The Jews looked for the coming One, not as a Savior from sin, but as a great prince who should bring all nations under the supremacy of the Lion of the tribe of Judah. In vain had John the Baptist called them to repentance.

In vain had he, beside the Jordan, pointed to Jesus as the "Lamb of God who takes away the sin of the world" (John 1:29). God was seeking to direct their minds to Isaiah's prophecy of the suffering Savior, but they would not hear.

Had the teachers and leaders in Israel yielded to His transforming grace, Jesus would have made them His ambassadors among the people. In Judea first the coming of the kingdom had been proclaimed, and the call to repentance had been given. In the act of driving out the desecrators from the Temple at Jerusalem, Jesus had announced Himself as the Messiah—the one who should cleanse the soul from the defilement of sin and make His people a holy temple for the Lord. But the Jewish leaders would not humble themselves to receive the lowly Teacher from Nazareth. Then it was that, leaving Judea, He entered upon His ministry in Galilee.

His work there had continued some months before the Sermon on the Mount was given. The message He had proclaimed throughout the land, "The kingdom of heaven is at hand" (Matthew 4:17), had arrested the attention of all classes, and had still further fanned the flame of their ambitious hopes. The fame of the new Teacher had spread beyond the limits of Palestine. Notwithstanding the attitude of the religious leaders, the feeling was widespread that this might be the hoped-for Deliverer. Great multitudes thronged the steps of Jesus, and the popular enthusiasm ran high.

The time had come for the disciples who had been most closely associated with Christ to unite more directly in His work, that these vast throngs might not be left uncared-for, as sheep without a shepherd. Some of these disciples had joined themselves to Him at the beginning of His ministry, and nearly all the twelve had been associated together as members of the family of Jesus. Yet they also, misled by the teaching of the rabbis, shared the popular expectation of an earthly kingdom. Already they had been perplexed and troubled that He made no effort to strengthen His cause by securing the support of the priests and rabbis, that He did nothing to establish His authority as an earthly king.

A great work was yet to be accomplished for these disciples before they would be prepared for the sacred trust that would be theirs when Jesus should ascend to heaven. Yet they had responded to the love of Christ, and, though they were slow to believe, Jesus saw in them those whom He could train and discipline for His great work. And now that they had been long enough with Him to establish, in a measure, their faith in the divine character of His mission, and the people also had received evidence of His power which they could not question, the way was prepared for a clear statement of the principles of His kingdom that would help them to comprehend its true nature.

Alone upon a mountain near the Sea of Galilee, Jesus had spent all night in prayer for these chosen ones. At the dawn He called them to Him, and, with words of prayer and instruction, laid His hands upon their heads in benediction, setting them apart to the gospel work. Then He went with them to the seaside, where in the early morning a great multitude had already begun to assemble.

Besides the usual crowd from the Galilean towns, there were great numbers from Judea, Jerusalem, Perea, and the half-heathen population of Decapolis. Others came from Idumea, away to the south of Judea, and from Tyre and Sidon, the Phoenician cities on the shore of the Mediterranean. "When they heard how many things [Jesus] was doing" (Mark 3:8) they "came to hear Him and be healed of their diseases. . . . Power went out from Him and healed them all" (Luke 6:17-19).

Then, as the narrow beach did not afford even standing room within reach of His voice for all who desired to hear Him, Jesus led the way back to the mountainside. Reaching a level space that afforded a pleasant gathering place for the vast assembly, He seated Himself upon the grass, and His disciples and the multitude followed His example.

As they sat upon the green hillside, awaiting the words of the divine Teacher, their hearts were filled with thoughts of future glory. There were scribes and Pharisees who looked forward to the day when they should have dominion over the hated Romans and possess the riches and splendor of the world's great empire. The poor peasants and fishermen hoped to hear the assurance that their wretched hovels, the scanty food, the life of toil, and the fear of want were to be exchanged for mansions of plenty and days of ease. In place of the one coarse garment which was their covering by day and their blanket at night, they hoped that Christ would give them the rich and costly robes of their conquerors.

All hearts thrilled with the proud hope that Israel was soon to be honored before the nations as the chosen of the Lord, and Jerusalem exalted as the head of a universal kingdom.

The Beatitudes

"Then He opened His mouth and taught them, saying: 'Blessed are the poor in spirit, for theirs is the kingdom of heaven.'" Matthew 5:2, 3.

As something strange and new, these words fall upon the ears of the wondering multitude. Such teaching is contrary to all they have ever heard from priest or rabbi. They see in it nothing to flatter their pride or to feed their ambitious hopes. But there is about this new Teacher a power that holds them spellbound. All feel instinctively that here is One who reads the secrets of the soul, yet who comes near to them with tender compassion. Their hearts open to Him. As they listen, the Holy Spirit unfolds to them something of the meaning of that lesson which humanity in all ages so needs to learn.

In the days of Christ the religious leaders of the people felt that they were rich in spiritual treasure. The prayer of the Pharisee, "God, I thank You that I am not like other men" (Luke 18:11), expressed the feeling of his class and, to a great degree, of the whole nation. But in the throng that surrounded Jesus there were some who had a sense of their spiritual poverty. They longed for "the grace of God that brings salvation" (Titus 2:11). In these souls, Christ's words of greeting awakened hope.

Jesus had presented the cup of blessing to those who felt that they were "rich" and "wealthy" (Revelation 3:17), and had need of nothing, and they had turned with scorn from the gracious gift. Those who feel whole, who think that they are reasonably good and are content with their condition, do not seek to become partakers of the grace and righteousness of Christ. Pride feels no need, and so it closes the heart against Christ and the infinite blessings He came to give. Those who know that they cannot possibly save themselves, or of themselves do any righteous action, are the ones who appreciate the help that Christ can bestow. They are the poor in spirit, whom He declares to be blessed.

Whom Christ pardons, He first makes penitent, and it is the office of the Holy Spirit to convince of sin. Those whose hearts have been moved by the convicting Spirit of God see that there is nothing good in themselves. They see that all they have ever done is mingled with self and sin. There is forgiveness for the penitent, because Christ is the "Lamb of God who takes away the sin of the world!" (John 1:29).

All who have a sense of their deep soul poverty, who feel that they have nothing good in themselves, may find righteousness and strength by looking to Jesus.

Of the poor in spirit Jesus says, "The kingdom of heaven belongs to them." This kingdom is not, as Christ's hearers had hoped, a temporal and earthly dominion. Christ was opening to the human race the spiritual kingdom of His love, His grace, His righteousness. His subjects are the poor in spirit, the meek, the persecuted for righteousness' sake. The kingdom of heaven is theirs. Though not yet fully accomplished, the work is begun in them which will make them "to be partakers of the inheritance of the saints in the light" (Colossians 1:12).

All who have a sense of their deep soul poverty, who feel that they have nothing good in themselves, may find righteousness and strength by looking to Jesus. We are not worthy of God's love, but Christ, our surety, is abundantly able to save all who come to Him. Whatever may have been your past experience, however discouraging your present circumstances, if you will come to Jesus just as you are, weak, helpless, and despairing, our compassionate Savior will meet you a great way off and will throw about you His arms of love and His robe of righteousness. He presents us to the Father clothed in the white raiment of His own character.

"Blessed are those who mourn, for they shall be comforted." Matthew 5:4.

The mourning here brought to view is true heart sorrow for sin. Jesus says, "I, if I am lifted up from the earth, will draw all peoples to Myself" (John 12:32). And as people are drawn to behold Jesus uplifted on the cross, they discern the sinfulness of humanity. They see that, while they have been loved with unspeakable tenderness, their lives have been a continual scene of ingratitude and rebellion. They have forsaken their best Friend and abused heaven's most precious gift. They are separated from God by a gulf of sin that is broad and black and deep, and they mourn in brokenness of heart.

Such mourning will be comforted. God reveals to us our guilt that we may flee to Christ, and through Him be set free from the bondage of sin. In true contrition we may come to the foot of the cross, and there leave our burdens.

The Savior's words have a message of comfort to those also who are suffering affliction or bereavement. God "does not afflict willingly, nor grieve the children of men" (Lamentations 3:33). When He permits trials and afflictions, it is "that we may be partakers of His holiness" (Hebrews 12:10). If received in faith, the cruel blow that blights the joys of earth will be the means of turning our eyes to heaven.

The trials of life are God's workers, to remove the impurities and roughness from our character. Their hewing, squaring, and chiseling, their burnishing and polishing, is a painful process. But the stone is brought forth prepared to fill its place in the heavenly temple. Upon no useless material does the Master bestow such careful, thorough work. Only His precious stones are polished after the similitude of a palace.

When tribulation comes upon us, how many of us are like Jacob! We think it the hand of an enemy. In the darkness we wrestle blindly until our strength is spent, and we find no comfort or deliverance. To Jacob the divine touch at break of day revealed the One with whom he had been contending—the Angel of the covenant. Weeping and helpless, he fell upon the breast of Infinite Love, to receive the blessing for which his soul longed. We also need to learn that trials mean benefit. To every stricken one, Jesus comes with the ministry of healing. The life of bereavement, pain, and suffering may be brightened by precious revealings of His presence.

God would not have us remain pressed down by speechless sorrow, with sore and breaking hearts. He would have us look up and behold His dear face of love. The blessed Savior stands by many whose eyes are so blinded by tears that they do not discern Him. He longs to clasp our hands, to have us look to Him in simple faith, permitting Him to guide us. His heart is open to our griefs, our sorrows, and our trials.

Blessed are they also who weep with Jesus in sympathy with the world's sorrow and in sorrow for its sin. Jesus was the Man of Sorrows, enduring heart anguish such as no language can portray. His spirit was torn and bruised by human transgression. He toiled with self-consuming zeal to relieve the wants and woes of humanity. His heart was heavy with sorrow as He saw multitudes refuse to come to Him that they might have life. All who are followers of Christ will share in this experience.

"For as the sufferings of Christ abound in us, so our consolation also abounds through Christ" (2 Corinthians 1:5). The Lord has special grace for the mourner, and its power is to melt hearts, to win souls. His love opens a channel into the wounded and bruised soul and becomes a healing balm to those who sorrow. "The Father of mercies and God of all comfort . . . comforts us in all our tribulation, that we may be able to comfort those who are in any trouble, with the comfort with which we ourselves are comforted by God" (verses 3, 4).

"Blessed are the meek." Matthew 5:5.

Throughout the Beatitudes there is an advancing line of Christian experience. Those who have felt their need of Christ, those who have mourned because of sin and have sat with Christ in the school of affliction, will learn meekness from the divine Teacher.

Patience and gentleness under wrong were not characteristics prized by the heathen or by the Jews. The statement made under the inspiration of the Holy Spirit that Moses was the meekest person upon the earth would not have been regarded by the people of his time as a commendation. It would rather have excited pity or contempt. But Jesus places meekness among the first qualifications for His kingdom. In His own life and character the divine beauty of this precious grace is revealed.

Jesus, the brightness of the Father's glory, "did not consider it robbery to be equal with God, but made Himself of no reputation, taking the form of a servant, and coming in the likeness of men" (Philippians 2:6, 7). Through all the lowly experiences of life He consented to pass, walking among humanity not as a king, to demand homage, but as one whose mission it was to serve others. There was in His manner no taint of bigotry, no cold austerity. The world's Redeemer had a greater than angelic nature, yet united with His divine majesty were meekness and humility that attracted all to Himself.

Jesus emptied Himself, and in all that He did, self did not appear. He subordinated all things to the will of His Father. When His mission on earth was about to close, He could say to His Father, "I have glorified You on the earth. I have finished the work which You have given Me to do" (John 17:4). And He bids us, "Learn from Me, for I am gentle and lowly in heart" (Matthew 11:29). Let self be dethroned and no longer hold the supremacy of the soul.

Human nature is ever struggling for expression, ready for contest. But he who learns of Christ is emptied of self, of pride, of love of supremacy. Then we are not anxious to have the highest place. We have no ambition to crowd and elbow ourselves into notice. Instead, we feel that our highest place is at the feet of our Savior. We look to Jesus, waiting for His hand to lead, listening for His voice to guide.

When we receive Christ as an abiding guest in the soul, the peace of God will keep our hearts and minds through Christ Jesus. The Savior's life on earth, though lived in the midst of conflict, was a life of peace. While angry enemies were constantly pursuing Him, He said, "He who sent Me is with Me. The Father has not left Me alone, for I always do those things that please Him" (John 8:29). No storm of human or satanic wrath could disturb the calm of that perfect communion with God. And He says to us, "Peace I leave with you, My peace I give to you" (John 14:27).

It is the love of self that destroys our peace. While self is all alive, we stand ready continually to guard it from mortification and insult. But when self is dead and our life is hid with Christ in God, we shall not take neglects or slights to heart. We shall be deaf to reproach and blind to scorn and insult.

Happiness drawn from earthly sources is as changeable as varying circumstances can make it; but the peace of Christ is a constant and abiding peace. It does not depend upon any circumstances in life, on the amount of worldly goods or the number of earthly friends. Christ is the fountain of living water, and happiness drawn from Him can never fail.

The meekness of Christ, manifested in the home, makes the family members happy, provokes no quarrel, gives back no angry answer, but soothes the irritated temper and diffuses a gentleness that is felt by all within its charmed circle. Wherever cherished, it makes the families of earth a part of the one great family above.

It was through the desire for self-exaltation that sin entered into the world, and our first parents lost the dominion over this fair earth, their kingdom. It is through self-abnegation that Christ redeems what was lost. And He says we are to overcome as He did (Revelation 3:21). Through humility and self-surrender we may become heirs with Him when "the meek shall inherit the earth" (Psalm 37:11).

The earth promised to the meek will not be like this present one, darkened with the shadow of death and the curse. "We, according to His promise, look for new heavens and a new earth in which righteousness dwells" (2 Peter 3:13).

There is no disappointment, no sorrow, no sin, no one who shall say, I am sick. There is no mourning, no death; there are no partings, no broken hearts. But Jesus is there. Peace is there. There "they shall neither hunger nor thirst, neither heat nor sun shall strike them; for He who has mercy on them will lead them, even by the springs of water He will guide them" (Isaiah 49:10).

"Blessed are those who hunger and thirst for righteousness,
for they shall be filled." Matthew 5:6.

Righteousness is holiness, likeness to God, and "God is love" (1 John 4:16). It is conformity to the law of God, "for all Your commandments are righteous" (Psalm 119:172) and "love is the fulfillment of the law" (Romans 13:10). Righteousness is love, and love is the light and the life of God. The righteousness of God is embodied in Christ. We receive righteousness by receiving Him.

Not by painful struggles or wearisome toil, not by gift or sacrifice, is righteousness obtained. Rather it is freely given to every soul who hungers and thirsts to receive it. "Everyone who thirsts, come to the waters; and you who have no money, come, buy and eat" "without money and without price" (Isaiah 55:1). "'Their righteousness is from Me,' says the Lord" (Isaiah 54:17), and "Now this is His name by which He will be called: THE LORD OUR RIGHTEOUSNESS" (Jeremiah 23:6).

No human agent can supply that which will satisfy the hunger and thirst of the soul. But Jesus says, "I stand at the door and knock. If anyone hears My voice and opens the door, I will come in to him and dine with him, and he with Me" (Revelation 3:20). "I am the bread of life. He who comes to Me shall never hunger, and he who believes in Me shall never thirst" (John 6:35).

As we need food to sustain our physical strength, so do we need Christ, the Bread from heaven, to sustain spiritual life and impart strength to work the works of God. As the body is continually receiving the nourishment that sustains life and vigor, so the soul must be constantly communing with Christ, submitting to Him and depending wholly upon Him.

As we discern the perfection of our Savior's character we shall desire to become wholly transformed and renewed in the image of His purity. The more we know of God, the higher will be our ideal of character and the more earnest our longing to reflect His likeness. A divine element combines with the human when the soul reaches out after God.

If you have a sense of need in your soul, if you hunger and thirst after righteousness, this is an evidence that Christ has worked upon your heart, in order that you may seek Him to do for you, through the endowment of the Holy Spirit, those things which it is impossible for you to do for yourself.

The words of God are the wellsprings of life. As you seek those living springs, you will, through the Holy Spirit, be brought into communion with Christ. Familiar truths will present themselves to your mind in a new aspect. Texts of Scripture will burst upon you with a new meaning, and you will know that Christ is leading you, that a divine Teacher is at your side.

As the Holy Spirit opens to you the truth, you will long to speak to others of the comforting things that have been revealed to you. When brought into association with others you will communicate some fresh thought in regard to the character or the work of Christ. You will have some fresh revelation of His pitying love to give both to those who love Him and to those who love Him not.

As you impart, you will receive in richer and more abundant measure. Every revelation of God to the soul increases the capacity to know and to love. The continual cry of the heart is "More of You," and ever the Spirit's answer is "Much more" (Romans 5:9, 10). For our God de-

11

lights to do "exceedingly abundantly above all that we ask or think" (Ephesians 3:20). To Jesus, who emptied Himself for the salvation of lost humanity, the Holy Spirit was given without measure. So it will be given to every follower of Christ when the whole heart is surrendered to His indwelling.

God has poured out His love unstintedly, as showers that refresh the earth. "When the poor and needy seek water, and there is none, and their tongues fail for thirst, I, the Lord, will hear them; I, the God of Israel, will not forsake them. I will open rivers in desolate heights, and fountains in the midst of the valleys; I will make the wilderness a pool of water, and the dry land springs of water" (Isaiah 41:17, 18).

"Blessed are the merciful, for they shall obtain mercy." Matthew 5:7.

The human heart is by nature cold and dark and unloving. Whenever people manifest a spirit of mercy and forgiveness, they do it not of themselves, but through the influence of the divine Spirit moving upon their hearts. "We love Him because He first loved us" (1 John 4:19).

God is Himself the source of all mercy. His name is "merciful and gracious" (Exodus 34:6). He does not treat us according to our desert. He does not ask if we are worthy of His love, but He pours upon us the riches of His love, to make us worthy. He is not vindictive. He seeks not to punish, but to redeem. It is true that God "by no means" clears the guilty (verse 7), but He would take away the guilt.

The merciful are "partakers of the divine nature" (2 Peter 1:4), and in them the compassionate love of God finds expression. All whose hearts are in sympathy with the heart of Infinite Love will seek to reclaim and not to condemn.

To the appeal of the erring, the tempted, the wretched victims of want and sin, Christians do not ask, Are they worthy? but, How can I benefit them? In the most wretched, the most debased, they see souls whom Christ died to save and for whom God has given to His children the ministry of reconciliation.

There are many to whom life is a painful struggle. Kind words, looks of sympathy, expressions of appreciation, would be to many a struggling and lonely one as a cup of cold water to a thirsty soul. A word of sympathy, an act of kindness, would lift burdens that rest heavily upon weary shoulders. And every word or deed of unselfish kindness is an expression of the love of Christ for lost humanity.

The merciful "shall obtain mercy." There is sweet peace for the compassionate spirit, a blessed satisfaction in the life of self-forgetful service for the good of others. The Holy Spirit that abides in the soul and is manifest in the life will soften hard hearts and awaken sympathy and tenderness. "Blessed is he who considers the poor; the Lord will deliver him in time of trouble. The Lord will preserve him and keep him alive" (Psalm 41:1, 2). And in the hour of final need the merciful shall find refuge in the mercy of the compassionate Savior.

"Blessed are the pure in heart, for they shall see God." Matthew 5:8.

The Jews were so exacting in regard to ceremonial purity that their regulations became extremely burdensome. Their minds were occupied with rules and restrictions and the fear of outward defilement, and they did not perceive the stain that selfishness and malice impart to the soul.

Jesus does not mention this ceremonial purity as one of the conditions for entering His kingdom, but points out the need of purity of heart. The wisdom that is from above "is first pure" (James 3:17). Into the city of God there will enter nothing that defiles. All who are to be dwellers there will here have become pure in heart. In one who is learning of Jesus, there will be displayed a growing distaste for careless manners, unseemly language, and coarse thought.

The Holy Spirit that abides in the soul and is manifest in the life will soften hard hearts and awaken sympathy and tenderness.

But the words of Jesus, "Blessed are the pure in heart," have a deeper meaning—not merely pure in the sense in which the world understands purity, free from that which is sensual, but true in the hidden purposes and motives of the soul, free from pride and self-seeking, humble, unselfish, childlike.

Only like can appreciate like. Unless you accept in your own life the principle of self-sacrificing love, which is the principle of His character, you cannot know God. The heart that is deceived by Satan looks upon God as a tyrannical, relentless being. The selfish characteristics of humanity, even of Satan himself, are attributed to the loving Creator. To the great mass of humanity, Christ Himself is "as a root out of dry ground," and they see in Him "no beauty" that they should "desire Him" (Isaiah 53:2). Even His disciples were so blinded by the selfishness of their hearts that they were slow to understand Him who had come to manifest to them the Father's love. He was understood fully in heaven alone.

When Christ shall come in His Glory, the wicked cannot endure to behold Him. They will pray to be hidden from the face of Him who died to redeem them.

But to hearts that have become purified through the indwelling of the Holy Spirit, all is changed. They can know God. By faith we behold Him here and now.

In our daily experience we discern His goodness and compassion in the manifestation of His providence. We recognize Him in the character of His Son. The Holy Spirit takes the truth concerning God and Him whom He sent, and opens it to the understanding and to the heart. The pure in heart see God in a new and endearing relation, as their Redeemer. They discern the purity and loveliness of His character and long to reflect His image. They see Him as a Father longing to embrace a repenting child, and their hearts are filled with joy unspeakable.

The pure in heart discern the Creator in the works of His mighty hand, in the things of beauty that comprise the universe. In His Written Word they read in clearer lines the revelation of His mercy, His goodness, and His grace. The beauty and preciousness of truth, which are undiscerned by the worldly-wise, are constantly unfolding to those who have a trusting, childlike desire to know and to do the will of God. The pure in heart live as in the visible presence of God, and they will see Him face to face in the future immortal state.

"Blessed are the peacemakers, for they shall be called sons of God."
Matthew 5:9.

Christ is the "Prince of Peace" (Isaiah 9:6). It is His mission to restore to earth and heaven the peace that sin has broken. "Therefore, having been justified by faith, we have peace with God through our Lord Jesus

Christ" (Romans 5:1). All those who consent to renounce sin and open the heart to the love of Christ become partakers of this heavenly peace.

There is no other ground of peace than this. The grace of Christ received into the heart, subdues enmity. It quells strife and fills the soul with love. The heart that is in harmony with God partakes of the peace of heaven and will diffuse its blessed influence on all around.

Christ's followers are sent to the world with the message of peace. Whoever, by the quiet, unconscious influence of a holy life, shall reveal the love of Christ—whoever, by word or deed, shall lead others to renounce sin and yield their hearts to God—is a peacemaker.

And "blessed are the peacemakers: for they shall be called the children of God" (KJV). The spirit of peace is evidence of their connection with heaven. The fragrance of the life, the loveliness of the character, reveal to the world that they are children of God. "Everyone who loves is born of God and knows God" (1 John 4:7).

"Blessed are those who are persecuted for righteousness' sake, for theirs is the kingdom of heaven." Matthew 5:10.

Jesus does not present to His followers the hope of attaining earthly glory and riches, of having a life free from trial, but He presents to them the privilege of walking with their Master in the paths of self-denial and reproach.

He who came to redeem the lost world was opposed by the united forces of the adversaries of God and humankind. In an unpitying confederacy, evil people and evil angels arrayed themselves against the Prince of Peace. Though His every word and act breathed of divine compassion, His unlikeness to the world provoked the bitterest hostility. So it is with all who will live godly in Christ Jesus. Between righteousness and sin, love and hatred, truth and falsehood, there is an irrepressible conflict. When men and women present the love of Christ and the beauty of holiness, they are drawing away the subjects of Satan's kingdom, and the prince of evil is aroused to resist it.

Principalities and powers and wicked spirits in high places are arrayed against all who yield obedience to the law of heaven. Therefore, persecution should bring joy to the disciples of Christ, for it is an evidence that they are following in the steps of their Master.

While the Lord has not promised His people exemption from trials, He has promised that which is far better. He has said, "My grace is sufficient for you, for My strength is made perfect in weakness" (2 Corinthians 12:9). If you are called to go through the fiery furnace for His sake, Jesus will be by your side even as He was with the faithful three in Babylon. Those who love their Redeemer will rejoice at every opportunity of sharing with Him humiliation and reproach.

In all ages Satan has persecuted the people of God. He has tortured them and put them to death, but in dying they became conquerors. They revealed in their steadfast faith a mightier One than Satan. Satan could torture and kill the body, but he could not touch the life hid with Christ in God. He could incarcerate in prison walls, but he could not bind the spirit. They could look beyond the gloom to the glory, saying, "The sufferings of this present time are not worthy to be compared with the glory which shall be revealed in us" (Romans 8:18).

Through trials and persecution, the glory—the character—of God is revealed in His chosen ones. The members of God's church, hated and persecuted by the world, are educated and disciplined in the school of Christ. They are purified in the furnace of affliction. They follow Christ through sore conflicts; they endure self-denial and experience bitter disappointments; but their painful experience teaches them the guilt and woe of sin, and they look on it with abhorrence. Being partakers of Christ's sufferings, they are destined to be partakers of His glory.

In holy vision the prophet saw the triumph of the people of God. He says, "I saw something like a sea of glass mingled with fire'" (Revelation 15:2). "These are the ones who come out of the great tribulation, and washed their robes and made them white in the blood of the Lamb. Therefore they are before the throne of God, and serve Him day and night in His temple. And He who sits on the throne will dwell among them" (Revelation 7:14, 15).

"Blessed are you when they revile and persecute you." Matthew 5:11.

Ever since his fall, Satan has worked by means of deception. As he has misrepresented God, so through his agents he misrepresents the children of God.

While slander may blacken the reputation, it cannot stain the character. That is in God's keeping. So long as we do not consent to sin, there is no power, whether human or satanic, that can bring a stain upon the soul. People whose hearts are stayed upon God are just the same in the hour of their most afflicting trials and most discouraging surroundings as when the light and favor of God seemed to be upon them. Their words, their motives, their actions, may be misrepresented and falsified, but like Moses, they endure as "seeing Him who is invisible" (Hebrews 11:27), looking not "at the things which are seen, but at the things which are not seen" (2 Corinthians 4:18).

When people "revile and persecute you," said Jesus, "rejoice and be exceedingly glad" (Matthew 5:11, 12). And He pointed His hearers to the prophets "who spoke in the name of the Lord, as an example of suffering and patience" (James 5:10).

In every age God's chosen messengers have been reviled and persecuted, yet through their affliction the knowledge of God has been spread abroad. God means that truth shall be brought to the front and become the subject of examination and discussion. The minds of the people must be agitated. Every controversy, every reproach, every effort to restrict liberty of conscience, is God's means of awakening minds that otherwise might slumber.

How often this result has been seen in the history of God's messengers! When the noble and eloquent Stephen was stoned to death at the instigation of the Sanhedrin council, there was no loss to the cause of the gospel. The light of heaven that glorified his face, the divine compassion breathed in his dying prayer, were as a sharp arrow of conviction to the bigoted Sanhedrist who stood by, and Saul, the persecuting Pharisee, became a chosen vessel to bear the name of Christ before Gentiles and kings and the children of Israel. And long afterward Paul the aged wrote from his prison house at Rome: "Some indeed preach Christ even from envy and strife," "supposing to add affliction to my chains. . . . What then? Only that in every way, whether in pretense or truth, Christ is preached; and in this I rejoice" (Philippians 1:15-18). Through Paul's imprisonment the gospel was spread abroad, and souls were won for Christ in the very palace of the Caesars.

Great is the reward in heaven of those who are witnesses for Christ through persecution and reproach. While the people are looking for earthly good, Jesus points them to a heavenly reward. But He does not place it all in the future life—it begins here. To know Him in whom dwells "all the fullness of the Godhead bodily" (Colossians 2:9)—to be brought into sympathy with Him, to know His love and power, to possess the unsearchable riches of Christ—"this is the heritage of the servants of the Lord" (Isaiah 54:17).

"You are the salt of the earth." Matthew 5:13.

Salt is valued for its preservative properties. When God calls His children salt, He would teach them that His purpose in making them the subjects of His grace is that they may become agents in saving others. The object of God in choosing a people was not only that He might adopt them as His sons and daughters, but that through them the world might receive the grace that brings salvation (Titus 2:11). When the Lord chose Abraham, it was not simply to be the special friend of God, but to be a medium of the privileges the Lord desired to bestow upon the nations. Jesus, in that last prayer with His disciples before His crucifixion, said, "For their sakes I sanctify Myself, that they also might be sanctified by the truth" (John 17:19). In like manner Christians who are purified through the truth will possess saving qualities that preserve the world from utter moral corruption.

Salt must be mingled with the substance to which it is added. It must penetrate and infuse in order to preserve. So it is through personal contact and association that human beings are reached by the saving power of the gospel. They are not saved in masses, but as individuals. Personal influence is a power. We must come close to those whom we desire to benefit.

The savor of the salt represents the vital power of the Christian—the love of Jesus in the heart, the righteousness of Christ pervading the life. Sincere believers diffuse vital energy that imparts new moral power to the souls for whom they labor. It is not human power but the power of the Holy Spirit that does the transforming work.

Jesus added the solemn warning: "If the salt loses its flavor, how shall it be seasoned? It is then good for nothing, but to be thrown out and trampled underfoot" (Matthew 5:13).

As they listened to the words of Christ, the people could see the white salt glistening in the pathways where it had been cast aside because it had lost its savor and was therefore useless. It well represented the condition of the Pharisees and the effect of their religion upon society. It represents the life of every soul from whom the power of the grace of God has departed and who has become cold and Christless.

Without a living faith in Christ as a personal Savior it is impossible to make our influence felt in a skeptical world. We cannot give to others that which we do not ourselves possess. It is in proportion to our own devotion and consecration to Christ that we exert an influence for the blessing and uplifting of humanity. If there is

> *When love fills the heart, it will flow out to others, not because of favors received from them, but because love is the principle of action.*

no actual service, no genuine love, no reality of experience, there is no power to help, no connection with heaven, no savor of Christ in the life. Unless the Holy Spirit can use us as agents through whom to communicate to the world the truth as it is in Jesus, we are as salt that has lost its savor and is entirely worthless.

When love fills the heart, it will flow out to others, not because of favors received from them, but because love is the principle of action. Love modifies the character, governs the impulses, subdues enmity, and ennobles the affections. Cherished in the heart, it sweetens the entire life and sheds its blessing upon all around. It is this, and this only, that can make us the salt of the earth.

"You are the light of the world." Matthew 5:14.

As Jesus taught the people, He made His lessons interesting and held the attention of His hearers by frequent illustrations from the scenes of nature about them. The people had come together while it was yet morning. The glorious sun, climbing higher and higher in the blue sky, was chasing away the shadows that lurked in the valleys and among the narrow ravines of the mountains. The sunlight flooded the land with its splendor. The placid surface of the lake reflected the golden light and mirrored the rosy clouds of morning.

The Savior looked upon those before Him, and then to the rising sun, and said to His disciples, "You are the light of the world." As the sun goes forth on its errand of love, dispelling the shades of night and awakening the world to life, so the followers of Christ are to go forth on their mission, diffusing the light of heaven upon those who are in the darkness of error and sin.

In the brilliant light of the morning, the towns and villages upon the surrounding hills stood out clearly. Pointing to them, Jesus said, "A city that is set upon a hill cannot be hidden" (verse 14). And He added, "Nor do they light a lamp and put it under a basket, but on a lampstand, and it gives light to all who are in the house" (verse 15). Most of those who listened to the words of Jesus were peasants and fishermen whose lowly dwellings contained but one room, in which the single lamp on its stand shone to all in the house. In like manner, said Jesus, "let your light so shine before men, that they may see your good works and glorify your Father in heaven" (verse 16).

No other light ever has shone or ever will shine upon fallen humanity save that which emanates from Christ. Jesus, the Savior, is the only light that can illuminate the darkness of a world lying in sin. Of Christ it is written, "In Him was life, and the life was the light of men" (John 1:4). It was by receiving of His life that His disciples could become light bearers. The life of Christ in the soul, His love revealed in the character, would make them the light of the world.

Humanity has in itself no light. Like the moon when its face is turned away from the sun, we have not a single ray of brightness to shed into the darkness of the world. But when we turn toward the Sun of Righteousness, when we come in touch with Christ, the whole soul is aglow with the brightness of the divine presence.

Christ's followers are to be more than *a* light in the midst of humanity. They are *the* light of the world. Jesus says to all who have named His name, You have given yourselves to Me, and I have given you to the world as My representatives. As the Father had sent Him into the world, so, He declares, "I also have sent them into the world" (John 17:18). As Christ is the channel for the revelation of the Father, so we are to be the channel for the revelation of Christ. While our Savior is the great source of illumination, He revealed Himself through humanity.

God's blessings are bestowed through human instrumentality. Humanity, united to the divine nature, must touch humanity. Angels of glory wait to communicate through you heaven's light and power to souls that are ready to perish.

But Jesus did not bid the disciples, "Strive to *make* your light shine." He said, *"Let* it shine." If Christ is dwelling in the heart, it is impossible to conceal the light of His presence. If those who profess to be followers of Christ are not the light of the world, it is because they have no connection with the Source of light.

In all ages the "Spirit of Christ who was in them" (1 Peter 1:11) has made God's true children the light of the people of their generation. Through them God was revealed to the world. In like manner the disciples of Christ are set as light bearers on the way to heaven. The divine love glowing in the heart, the Christlike harmony manifested in the life, are as a glimpse of heaven granted to the world.

It is thus that human beings are led to believe "the love that God has for us" (1 John 4:16). Thus hearts once sinful and corrupt are purified and transformed, to be presented "faultless before the presence of His glory with exceeding joy" (Jude 24).

The Savior's words, "You are the light of the world," point to the fact that He has committed to His followers a worldwide mission. The words that the people were hearing from His lips were unlike anything to which they had ever listened from priest or rabbi. Christ tears away the self-love, the dividing prejudice of nationality, and teaches a love for all the human family. He abolishes all territorial lines and artificial distinctions of society. He makes no difference between neighbors and strangers, friends and enemies. He teaches us to look upon every needy soul as our neighbor.

As the rays of the sun penetrate to the remotest corners of the globe, so God designs that the members of the church shall scatter into all lands, letting the light of Christ shine out from them.

It is thus that God's purpose in calling His people, from Abraham on the plains of Mesopotamia to us in this age, is to reach its fulfillment. He says, "I will bless you. . . ; and you shall be a blessing" (Genesis 12:2). The words of Christ through the gospel prophet, which are but reechoed in the Sermon on the Mount, are for us in this last generation: "Arise, shine; for your light has come! And the glory of the Lord is risen upon you" (Isaiah 60:1).

Christ accepts, oh, so gladly, every human agency that is surrendered to Him. He brings the human into union with the divine, that He may communicate to the world the mysteries of incarnate love. Talk it, pray it, sing it—proclaim abroad the message of His glory, and keep pressing onward to the regions beyond.

The Spirituality of the Law

"I did not come to destroy but to fulfill." Matthew 5:17.

It was Christ who, amid thunder and flame, had proclaimed the law upon Mount Sinai. The glory of God, like devouring fire, rested upon its summit, and the mountain quaked at the presence of the Lord. The hosts of Israel, lying prostrate upon the earth, had listened in awe to the sacred precepts of the law. What a contrast to the scene upon the mount of the Beatitudes! Under the summer sky, with no sound to break the stillness but the song of birds, Jesus unfolded the principles of His kingdom. Yet He who spoke to the people that day in accents of love was opening to them the principles of the law proclaimed upon Sinai.

When the law was given, Israel, degraded by the long bondage in Egypt, needed to be impressed with the power and majesty of God; yet He revealed Himself to them no less as a God of love.

"The Lord came from Sinai,
    And dawned on them from Seir;
He shone forth from Mount Paran,
    And He came with ten thousands of saints;

From His right hand came a fiery law for them.
Yes, He loves the people;
All His saints are in Your hand;
They sit down at Your feet;
Everyone receives Your words" (Deuteronomy 33:2, 3).

It was to Moses that God revealed His glory in those wonderful words that have been the treasured heritage of the ages: "The Lord, the Lord God, merciful and gracious, longsuffering, and abounding in goodness and truth, keeping mercy for thousands, forgiving iniquity and transgression and sin" (Exodus 34:6, 7).

The law given upon Sinai was the enunciation of the principle of love, a revelation to earth of the law of heaven. It was ordained in the hand of a Mediator—spoken by Him through whose power human hearts could be brought into harmony with its principles. God had revealed the purpose of the law when He declared to Israel, "You shall be holy . . . to Me" (Exodus 22:31).

But Israel had not perceived the spiritual nature of the law. Too often their professed obedience was but an observance of forms and ceremonies, rather than a surrender of the heart to the sovereignty of love. As Jesus in His character and work represented to humanity the holy, benevolent, and paternal attributes of God, and presented the worthlessness of mere ceremonial obedience, the Jewish leaders did not accept or understand His words. They thought that He dwelt too lightly upon the requirements of the law. When He set before them the very truths that were the soul of their divinely appointed service, they, looking only at the external, accused Him of seeking to overthrow it.

The words of Christ, though calmly spoken, were uttered with an earnestness and power that stirred the hearts of the people. They "were astonished at His teaching, for He taught them as one having authority, and not as the scribes" (Matthew 7:28, 29). The Pharisees noted the vast difference between their manner of instruction and that of Christ. They saw that the majesty and purity and beauty of the truth, with its deep and gentle influence, was taking firm hold upon many minds. The Savior's divine love and tenderness drew hearts to Him. The rabbis saw that by His teaching the whole tenor of the instruction they had given to the people was set at nought. They feared that He would draw the people entirely away from them.

On the mount, Jesus was closely watched by spies. As He unfolded the principles of righteousness, the Pharisees caused it to be whispered about that His teaching was in opposition to the precepts that God had given from Sinai. The Savior said nothing to unsettle faith in the religion and institutions that had been given through Moses. Every ray of divine light that Israel's great leader communicated to his people was received from Christ. While many are saying in their hearts that He has come to do away with the law, Jesus in unmistakable language reveals His attitude toward the divine statutes. "Do not think," He said, "that I came to destroy the Law or the Prophets" (Matthew 5:17).

It is the Creator, the Giver of the law, who declares that it is not His purpose to set aside its precepts. Everything in nature, from the mote in the sunbeam to the worlds on high, is under law. And upon obedience to these laws the order and harmony of the natural world depend. So there are great principles of righteousness to control the life of all intelligent beings, and upon conformity to these principles the well-being of the universe depends. Before this earth was called into being, God's law existed. Angels are governed by its principles, and in order for earth to be in harmony with heaven, humanity also must obey the divine statutes. The mission of Christ on earth was not to destroy the law, but by His grace to bring humanity back to obedience to its precepts.

Speaking of the law, Jesus said, "I did not come to destroy but to fulfill" (Matthew 5:17). He here used the word "fulfill" in the same sense as when He declared to John the Baptist His purpose to "fulfill all righteousness" (Matthew 3:15)—that is, to fill up the measure of the law's requirement, to give an example of perfect conformity to the will of God.

His mission was to "magnify the law and make it honorable" (Isaiah 42:21). He was to show the spiritual nature of the law, to present its far-reaching principles, and to make plain its eternal obligation.

The divine beauty of the character of Christ was a living representation of the character of the law of God. In His life it is made manifest that heaven-born love, Christlike principles, underlie the laws of eternal rectitude.

"Till heaven and earth pass away," said Jesus, "one jot or one tittle will by no means pass from the law till all is fulfilled" (Matthew 5:18). By His own obedience to the law, Christ testified to its immutable character and proved that through His grace it could be perfectly obeyed by every son and daughter of Adam. On the mount He declared that not the smallest iota should pass from the law till all things should be accomplished—all things that concern the human race, all that relates to the plan of redemption. He does not teach that the law is ever to be abrogated. So long as heaven and earth continue, the holy principles of God's law will remain.

Because the law of the Lord is perfect, and therefore changeless, it is impossible for sinful people, in themselves, to meet the standard of its requirement. This was why Jesus came as our Redeemer. It was His mission, by making human beings partakers of the divine nature, to bring them into harmony with the principles of the law of heaven. When we forsake our sins and receive Christ as our Savior, the law is exalted. The apostle Paul asks, "Do we then make void the law through faith? Certainly not! On the contrary, we establish the law" (Romans 3:31).

The new-covenant promise is "I will put My laws into their hearts, and in their minds I will write them" (Hebrews 10:16). While the system of types which pointed to Christ as the Lamb of God that should take away the sin of the world was to pass away at His death, the principles of righteousness embodied in the Decalogue are as immutable as the eternal throne. Not one command has been annulled, not a jot or tittle has been changed.

"All His precepts are sure. They stand fast forever and ever, and are done in truth and uprightness" (Psalm 111:7, 8).

"Whoever . . . breaks one of the least of these commandments, and teaches men so, shall be called least in the kingdom of heaven."
Matthew 5:19.

That is, he or she shall have no place in the kingdom. For those who willfully break one commandment do not, in spirit and truth, keep any of them. "Whoever shall keep the whole law, and yet stumble in one point, he is guilty of all" (James 2:10).

It is not the greatness of the act of disobedience that constitutes sin, but the fact of variance from God's expressed will in the least particular. This shows that the heart is divided in its service. There is a virtual denial of God, a rebellion against the laws of His government.

Whenever human beings choose their own way, they place themselves in conflict with God. They will have no place in the kingdom of heaven, for they are at war with the very principles of heaven. In disregarding the will of God they are placing themselves on the side of Satan, the enemy of God and humanity. Not by one word, not by many words, but by every word that God has spoken, are we to live. We cannot disregard one word, however trifling it may seem to us, and be safe. There is not a commandment of the law that is not for our good and happiness. In obedience to God's law, we are surrounded as with a hedge. Those who break down this divinely erected barrier at even one point have destroyed its power to protect them, for they have opened a way by which the enemy can enter to bring waste and ruin.

> *Not by one word, not by many words, but by every word that God has spoken, are we to live.*

By venturing to disregard the will of God upon one point, our first parents opened the floodgates of woe upon the world. And every individual who follows their example will reap a similar result. The love of God underlies every precept of His law, and those who depart from the commandment are working their own unhappiness and ruin.

"Unless your righteousness exceeds the righteousness of the scribes and Pharisees, you will by no means enter the kingdom of heaven." Matthew 5:20.

The scribes and Pharisees had accused not only Christ but His disciples as being sinners because of their disregard of the rabbinical rites and observances. Often the disciples had been perplexed and troubled by censure and accusation from those whom they had been accustomed to revere as religious teachers. Jesus declared that the righteousness upon which the Pharisees set so great value was worthless. The Jewish nation had claimed to be the special, loyal people who were favored of God, but Christ represented their religion as devoid of saving faith. All their pretensions of piety, their ceremonies, and even their boasted performance of the outward requirements of the law could not make them holy. They were not pure in heart or noble and Christlike in character.

A legal religion is insufficient to bring the soul into harmony with God. The hard, rigid orthodoxy of the Pharisees, destitute of contrition, tenderness, or love, was only a stumbling block to sinners. They were like the salt that had lost its savor, for their influence had no power to preserve the world from corruption. The only true faith is that faith "working through love" (Galatians 5:6) to purify the soul. It is as leaven that transforms the character.

All this the Jews should have learned from the teachings of the prophets. Centuries before, the cry of the soul for justification with God had found voice and answer in the words of the prophet Micah: "With what shall I come before the Lord, and bow myself before the High God? Shall I come before Him with burnt offerings, with calves a year old? Will the Lord be pleased with thousands of rams or ten thousand rivers of oil? . . . He has shown you . . . what is good; and what does the Lord require of you but to do justly, to love mercy, and to walk humbly with your God?" (Micah 6:6-8).

The prophet Hosea had pointed out what constitutes the very essence of Pharisaism, in the words "Israel . . . brings forth fruit for himself" (Hosea 10:1). In their professed service to God, the Jews were really working for self. Their righteousness was the fruit of their own efforts to keep the law according to their own ideas and for their own selfish benefit. Hence it could be no better than they were. In their endeavor to make themselves holy, they were trying to bring a clean thing out of an unclean.

The law of God is as holy as He is holy, as perfect as He is perfect. It presents to human beings the righteousness of God. It is impossible for people, of themselves, to keep this law, for human nature is depraved, deformed, and wholly unlike the character of God. The works of the selfish heart are "an unclean thing"; and "all our righteousnesses are like filthy rags" (Isaiah 64:6).

If they would enter the kingdom of heaven, the disciples of Christ must obtain righteousness of a different character from that of the Pharisees. God offered them, in His Son, the perfect righteousness of the law. If they would open their hearts fully to receive Christ, then the very life of God, His love, would dwell in them, transforming them into His own likeness. Through God's free gift they would possess the righteousness which the law requires.

Jesus proceeded to show His hearers what it means to keep the commandments of God—that it is a reproduction in themselves of the character of Christ. For in Him, God was daily made manifest before them.

> *"Whoever is angry with his brother without a cause*
> *shall be in danger of the judgment." Matthew 5:22.*

Through Moses the Lord had said, "You shall not hate your brother in your heart. . . . You shall not take vengeance, nor bear any grudge against the children of your people, but you shall love your neighbor as yourself" (Leviticus 19:17, 18). The truths that Christ presented were the same that had been taught by the prophets, but they had become obscured through hardness of heart and love of sin.

The Savior's words revealed to His hearers the fact that, while they were condemning others as transgressors, they were themselves equally guilty, for they were cherishing malice and hatred.

The spirit of hatred and revenge originated with Satan. It led him to put to death the Son of God. Whoever cherishes malice or unkindness is cherishing the same spirit. In the revengeful thought the evil deed lies enfolded, as the plant in the seed. "Whoever hates his brother is a murderer, and you know that no murderer has eternal life abiding in him" (1 John 3:15).

"Whoever says to his brother, 'Raca!' [vain fellow] shall be in danger of the council" (Matthew 5:22). In the gift of His Son for our redemption, God has shown how high a value He places upon every human soul, and He gives no one liberty to speak contemptuously of another. We shall see faults and weaknesses in those about us, but God claims every soul as His property—His by creation, and doubly His as purchased by the precious blood of Christ. All were created in His image, and even the most degraded are to be treated with respect and tenderness. God will hold us accountable for even a word spoken in contempt of one soul for whom Christ laid down His life.

Christ Himself, when contending with Satan about the body of Moses, "dared not bring against him a reviling accusation" (Jude 9). Had He done this, He would have placed Himself on Satan's ground, for accusation is the weapon of the evil one. He is called, in Scripture, "the accuser of our brethren" (Revelation 12:10). Jesus would employ none of Satan's weapons. He met him with the words "The Lord rebuke you" (Jude 9).

His example is for us. We are to leave with God the work of judging and condemning.

"Be reconciled to your brother." Matthew 5:24.

The love of God is a positive and active principle, a living spring, ever flowing to bless others. If the love of Christ dwells in us, we shall not only cherish no hatred toward others, but we shall seek in every way to manifest love toward them.

Jesus said, "If you bring your gift to the altar, and there remember that your brother has something against you, leave your gift there before the altar, and go your way. First be reconciled to your brother, and then come and offer your gift" (Matthew 5:23, 24). The sacrificial offerings expressed faith that through Christ the offerer had become a partaker of the mercy and love of God. But for one to express faith in God's pardoning love while indulging an unloving spirit would be a mere farce.

When people who profess to serve God wrong or injure another, they misrepresent the character of God to that person. The wrong must be confessed, and they must acknowledge it to be sin, in order to be in harmony with God. The other person may have done a greater wrong to us than we have done to them, but this does not lessen our responsibility to go to the individual with whom we are at odds, and in humility confess our sin and ask to be forgiven.

If we have in any manner defrauded or injured someone, we should make restitution. If we have unwittingly borne false witness, if we have misstated their words or injured their influence in any way, we should go to the people with whom we have conversed about them, and take back all our injurious misstatements.

If matters of difficulty between believers were not laid open before others but frankly spoken of between themselves in the spirit of Christian love, how much evil might be prevented! How many roots of bitterness whereby many are defiled would be destroyed, and how closely and tenderly might the followers of Christ be united in His love!

"Whoever looks at a woman to lust for her has already committed adultery with her in his heart." Matthew 5:28.

The Jews prided themselves on their morality and looked with horror upon the sensual practices of the heathen. The presence of the Roman officers whom the imperial rule had brought into Palestine was a continual offense to the people, for with these foreigners had come in a flood of heathen customs, lust, and dissipation. The people expected to hear from Jesus a stern denunciation of this class, but what was their astonishment as they listened to words that laid bare the evil of their own hearts! Those who find pleasure in dwelling upon scenes of impurity, who indulge the evil thought, the lustful look, may behold in the open sin, with its burden of shame and heartbreaking grief, the true nature of the evil which they have hidden in the chambers of their own soul. As a person "thinks in his heart, so is he" (Proverbs 23:7), for out of the heart "spring the issues of life" (Proverbs 4:23).

"If your right hand causes you to sin, cut it off and cast it from you." Matthew 5:30.

To prevent disease from spreading to the body and destroying life, people would submit to part even with their right hand. Much more should they be willing to surrender that which imperils the life of the soul.

Only through the surrender of our will to God is it possible for Him to impart life to us.

God's purpose is not merely to deliver us from the suffering that is the inevitable result of sin, but to save us from sin itself. The soul, corrupted and deformed, is to be purified, transformed, and "conformed to the image of His Son" (Romans 8:29). Eternity alone can reveal the glorious destiny to which human beings, restored to God's image, may attain.

In order for us to reach this high ideal, that which causes the soul to stumble must be sacrificed. It is through the will that sin retains its hold upon us. The surrender of the will is represented as plucking out the eye or cutting off the hand. Often it seems to us that to surrender the will to God is to consent to go through life maimed or crippled. But it is better, says Christ, for self to be maimed, wounded, crippled, if thus you may enter into life. That which you look upon as disaster is the door to highest benefit.

God is the fountain of life, and we can have life only as we are in com-

30

munion with Him. Separated from God, existence may be ours for a little time, but we do not possess life. Only through the surrender of our will to God is it possible for Him to impart life to us. Only by receiving His life through self-surrender is it possible, said Jesus, for these hidden sins, which I have pointed out, to be overcome.

If you cling to self, refusing to yield your will to God, you are choosing death. To sin, wherever found, God is a consuming fire. If you choose sin, and refuse to separate from it, the presence of God, which consumes sin, must consume you.

It will require a sacrifice to give yourself to God, but it is a sacrifice of the lower for the higher, the earthly for the spiritual, the perishable for the eternal. God does not design that our will should be destroyed, for it is only through its exercise that we can accomplish what He would have us do. Our will is to be yielded to Him, that we may receive it again, purified and refined, and so linked in sympathy with the Divine that He can pour through us the tides of His love and power.

Not until he fell crippled and helpless upon the breast of the covenant angel did Jacob know the victory of conquering faith and receive the title of a prince with God. So Christ, the Captain of our salvation, was made "perfect through sufferings" (Hebrews 2:10), and the children of faith "out of weakness were made strong," and "turned to flight the armies of the aliens" (Hebrews 11:34).

"Is it lawful for a man to divorce his wife?" Matthew 19:3.

In the Sermon on the Mount Jesus declared plainly that there could be no dissolution of the marriage tie, except for unfaithfulness to the marriage vow. "Whoever divorces his wife, except for sexual immorality, and marries another, commits adultery" (verse 9).

When the Pharisees afterward questioned Him concerning the lawfulness of divorce, Jesus pointed His hearers back to the marriage institution as ordained at creation. He referred them to the blessed days of Eden, when God pronounced all things "very good." Then marriage and the Sabbath had their origin, twin institutions for the glory of God in the benefit of humanity. Then, as the Creator joined the hands of the holy pair in wedlock, saying, "A man shall leave his father and mother and be joined to his wife, and they shall become one flesh" (Genesis 2:24). He enunciated the law of marriage for all the children of Adam to the close of time.

Like every other one of God's good gifts entrusted to the keeping of humanity, marriage has been perverted by sin; but it is the purpose of the gospel to restore its purity and beauty. In both the Old and the New Testament the marriage relation is employed to represent the tender and sacred union that exists between Christ and His people, the redeemed ones whom He has purchased at the cost of Calvary. "Your Maker is your husband" (Isaiah 54:5). "I am married to you" (Jeremiah 3:14).

In later times Paul the apostle, writing to the Ephesian Christians, declares that the Lord has constituted the husband the head of the wife, to be her protector, the house-band, binding the members of the family together, even as Christ is the head of the church and the Savior of the mystical body. "Husbands, love your wives, just as Christ also loved the church and gave Himself for her, that He might sanctify and cleanse her with the washing of water by the word, that He might present her to Himself a glorious church, not having spot or wrinkle or any such thing, but that she should be holy and without blemish. So husbands ought to love their own wives as their own bodies" (Ephesians 5:25-28).

Now, as in Christ's day, the condition of society presents a sad comment upon heaven's ideal of this sacred relation. Yet even for those who have found bitterness and disappointment where they had hoped for companionship and joy, the gospel of Christ offers a solace. The patience and gentleness which His Spirit can impart will sweeten the bitter lot. And through the surrender of the soul to God, His wisdom can accomplish what human wisdom fails to do. Through the revelation of His grace, hearts that were once indifferent or estranged may be united in bonds that are firmer and more enduring than those of earth—the golden bonds of a love that will bear the test of trial.

"Do not swear at all." Matthew 5:34.

The reason for this command is given: We are not to swear "by heaven, for it is God's throne; nor by the earth, for it is His footstool; nor by Jerusalem, for it is the city of the great King. Nor shall you swear by your head, because you cannot make one hair white or black" (verses 34-36).

The Jews understood the third commandment as prohibiting the profane use of the name of God, but they thought themselves at liberty to employ other oaths. Oath taking was common among them. Through Moses they had been forbidden to swear falsely, but they had many devices for freeing themselves from the obligation imposed by an oath. They did not fear to indulge in what was really profanity, nor did they shrink from per- jury so long as it was veiled by some technical evasion of the law.

Jesus condemned their practices, declaring that their custom of oath taking was a transgression of the commandment of God. Our Savior did not, however, forbid the use of the judicial oath, in which God is solemnly called to witness that what is said is truth and nothing but the truth. Jesus Himself, at His trial before the Sanhedrin, did not refuse to testify under oath. The high priest said unto Him, "I put You under oath by the living God. Tell us if You are the Christ, the Son of God!" (Matthew 26:63). Jesus answered, "It is as you said" (verse 64). Had Christ in the Sermon on the Mount condemned the judicial oath, He would at His trial have reproved the high priest and thus, for the benefit of His followers, have enforced His own teaching.

There are very many who do not fear to deceive their associates and companions, but they have been taught, and have been impressed by the Spirit of God, that it is a fearful thing to lie to their Maker. When put under oath they are made to feel that they are not testifying merely be- fore human beings, but before God; that if they bear false witness, it is to Him who reads the heart and who knows the exact truth. The knowl- edge of the fearful judgments that have followed this sin has a restraining influence upon them.

But if there is anyone who can consistently testify under oath, it is the Christian. Christians live constantly as in the presence of God, know- ing that every thought is open to His eyes. When Christians are required to do so in a lawful manner, it is right for them to appeal to God as a wit- ness that what they say is the truth and nothing but the truth.

Jesus proceeded to lay down a principle that would make oath tak- ing needless. He teaches that the exact truth should be the law of speech. "Let your 'Yes' be 'Yes,' and your 'No,' 'No.' For whatever is more than these is from the evil one" (Matthew 5:37).

These words condemn all those meaningless phrases and expletives that border on profanity. They condemn the deceptive compliments, the eva- sion of truth, the flattering phrases, the exaggerations, the misrepresentations in trade, that are current in society and in the business world. They teach that people who try to appear what they are not, or whose words do not convey the real sentiment of the heart, cannot be called truthful.

Everything that Christians do should be as transparent as the sunlight. Truth is from God. Deception, in every one of its myriad forms, is from Satan. And those who in any way depart from the straight line of truth are betraying themselves into the power of the wicked one. Yet it is not a light or an easy thing to speak the exact truth. We cannot speak the truth unless we know the truth. How often preconceived opinions, mental bias, imperfect knowledge, errors of judgment, prevent a right understanding of matters! We cannot speak the truth unless our minds are continually guided by Him who is truth.

Through the apostle Paul, Christ bids us, "Let no corrupt communication proceed out of your mouth, but what is good for necessary edification, that it may impart grace to the hearers" (Ephesians 4:29). In the light of this scripture the words of Christ upon the mount are seen to condemn jesting, trifling, and unchaste conversation. They require that our words should be not only truthful but pure.

Those who have learned of Christ will "have no fellowship with the unfruitful works of darkness" (Ephesians 5:11). In speech, as in life, they will be straightforward and true, for they are preparing for the fellowship of those holy ones in whose mouth "was found no deceit" (Revelation 14:5).

"I tell you not to resist an evil person. But whoever slaps you on your right cheek, turn the other to him also." Matthew 5:39.

Occasions of irritation to the Jews were constantly arising from their contact with the Roman soldiery. Collisions between the people and the soldiers were frequent, and these inflamed the popular hatred. Often as some Roman official with his guard of soldiers hastened from point to point, he would seize the Jewish peasants who were laboring in the field and compel them to carry burdens up the mountainside or render any other service that might be needed. This was in accordance with the Roman law and custom, and resistance to such demands only called forth taunts and cruelty.

Every day deepened in the hearts of the people the longing to cast off the Roman yoke. Especially among the bold, rough-handed Galileans the spirit of insurrection was rife. Capernaum, being a border town, was the seat of a Roman garrison, and even while Jesus was teaching, the sight of a company of soldiers recalled to His hearers the bitter thought of Israel's humiliation. The people looked eagerly to Christ, hoping that He was the one who was to humble the pride of Rome.

With sadness Jesus looks into the upturned faces before Him. He notes the spirit of revenge and knows how bitterly the people long to crush their oppressors. Mournfully He bids them, "I tell you not to resist an evil person. But whoever slaps you on your right cheek, turn the other to him also."

These words were but a reiteration of the teaching of the Old Testament. It is true that the rule "eye for eye, tooth for tooth" (Leviticus 24:20) was a provision in the laws given through Moses, but it was a civil statute. None were justified in avenging themselves, for they had the words of the Lord: "Do not say, 'I will recompense evil'" (Proverbs 20:22). "Do not say, 'I will do to him just as he has done to me'" (Proverbs 24:29). "Do not rejoice when your enemy falls" (verse 17). "If your enemy is hungry, give him bread to eat; and if he is thirsty, give him water to drink" (Proverbs 25:21).

The whole earthly life of Jesus was a manifestation of this principle. It was to bring the bread of life to His enemies that our Savior left His home in heaven. Though insults and persecution were heaped upon Him from the cradle to the grave, they called forth from Him only the expression of forgiving love. And from the cross of Calvary there

Those who are imbued with the Spirit of Christ abide in Christ. The blow that is aimed at them falls upon the Savior, who surrounds them with His presence.

come down through the ages His prayer for His murderers and the message of hope to the dying thief.

The Father's presence encircled Christ. Nothing befell Him but that which infinite love permitted for the blessing of the world. Here was His source of comfort, and it is for us. Those who are imbued with the Spirit of Christ abide in Christ. The blow that is aimed at them falls upon the Savior, who surrounds them with His presence. Nothing can touch them except by our Lord's permission, and "all things" that are permitted "work together for good to those who love God" (Romans 8:28).

"If anyone wants to sue you and take away your tunic, let him have your cloak also. And whoever compels you to go one mile, go with him two" (Matthew 5:40, 41).

Jesus bade His disciples, instead of resisting the demands of those in authority, to do even more than was required of them. So far as possible, they should discharge every obligation, even if it were beyond what the law of the land required. The law, as given through Moses, enjoined a careful concern for the poor. When poor people gave their garment as a pledge, or as security for a debt, creditors were not permitted to enter the dwelling to obtain it. They had to wait in the street for the pledge to be brought to them. And whatever the circumstances, the pledge had to be returned to its owner at nightfall (Deuteronomy 24:10-13).

In the days of Christ these merciful provisions were little regarded, but Jesus taught His disciples to submit to the decision of the court, even though this should demand more than the law of Moses authorized. Though it should demand a part of their clothing, they were to yield. More than this, they were to give to creditors their due, if necessary surrendering even more than the court gave them authority to seize.

Jesus added, "Give to him who asks you, and from him who wants to borrow from you do not turn away" (Matthew 5:42). Christ does not teach us to give indiscriminately to all who ask for charity, but says, "Willingly lend him . . . whatever he needs." This is to be a gift, rather than a loan, for we are to "lend, hoping for nothing in return" (Luke 6:35).

"Who gives himself with his alms feeds three,
  Himself, his hungering neighbor, and Me."

"Love your enemies." Matthew 5:44.

The Savior's lesson "I tell you not to resist an evil person" (verse 39) was a hard saying for the revengeful Jews, and they murmured against it among themselves. But Jesus now made a still stronger declaration: "You have heard that it was said, 'You shall love your neighbor and hate your enemy.' But I say to you, love your enemies, bless those who curse you, do good to those who hate you, and pray for those who spitefully use you and persecute you, that you may be sons of your Father in heaven" (verses 43-45).

36

Jesus pointed His hearers to the Ruler of the universe, under the new name "Our Father." He would have them understand how tenderly the heart of God yearned over them. He teaches that God cares for every lost soul—that "as a father pities his children" so "the Lord pities those who fear him" (Psalm 103:13). Such a conception of God was never given to the world by any religion but that of the Bible. Paganism teaches people to look upon the Supreme Being as an object of fear rather than of love—a malign deity to be appeased by sacrifices, rather than a Father pouring upon His children the gift of His love. Even the people of Israel had become so blinded to the precious teaching of the prophets concerning God that this revelation of His paternal love was as a new gift to the world.

The Jews held that God loved those who served Him—according to their view, those who fulfilled the requirements of the rabbis. All the rest of the world lay under His frown and curse. Not so, said Jesus. The whole world—the evil and the good—lies in the sunshine of His love. This truth you should have learned from nature itself, for God "makes His sun rise on the evil and on the good, and sends rain on the just and on the unjust" (Matthew 5:45).

It is not because of inherent power that year by year the earth produces its bounties and continues its motion around the sun. The hand of God guides the planets and keeps them in position in their orderly march through the heavens. It is through His power that summer and winter, seedtime and harvest, day and night, follow each other in their regular succession. It is by His word that vegetation flourishes, that the leaves appear and the flowers bloom. Every good thing we have, each ray of sunshine and shower of rain, every morsel of food, every moment of life, is a gift of love.

While we were yet unloving and unlovely in character, "hateful and hating one another" (Titus 3:3), our heavenly Father had mercy on us. "But when the kindness and love of God our Savior toward man appeared, not by works of righteousness which we have done, but according to His mercy He saved us" (verse 4). His love received will make us, in like manner, kind and tender, not merely toward those who please us, but to the most faulty and erring and sinful.

The children of God are those who are partakers of His nature. To be kind to the unthankful and to the evil, to do good hoping for nothing again, is the insignia of the royalty of heaven, the sure token by which the children of the Highest reveal their high estate.

"Therefore you shall be perfect, just as your Father in heaven is perfect."
Matthew 5:48.

The word "therefore" implies a conclusion, an inference from what has gone before. Jesus has been describing to His hearers the unfailing mercy and love of God, and He bids them therefore to be perfect. Because your heavenly Father "is kind to the unthankful and evil" (Luke 6:35), because He has stooped to lift you up, therefore, said Jesus, you may become like Him in character, and stand without fault in the presence of both human beings and angels.

The conditions of eternal life, under grace, are just what they were in Eden—perfect righteousness, harmony with God, perfect conformity to the principles of His law. The standard of character presented in the Old Testament is the same that is presented in the New Testament. This standard is not one to which we cannot attain. In every command or injunction that God gives there is a promise, the most positive, underlying the command. God has made provision that we may become like unto Him, and He will accomplish this for all who do not interpose a perverse will and thus frustrate His grace.

With untold love our God has loved us, and our love awakens toward Him as we comprehend something of the length and breadth and depth and height of His love. By the revelation of the attractive loveliness of Christ, by the knowledge of His love expressed to us while we were yet sinners, the stubborn heart is melted and subdued, and the sinner is transformed and becomes a child of heaven. God does not employ compulsory measures. Love is the agent which He uses to expel sin from the heart. By it He changes pride into humility, and enmity and unbelief into love and faith.

The Jews had been wearily toiling to reach perfection by their own efforts, and they had failed. Christ had already told them that their righteousness could never enter the kingdom of heaven. Now He points out to them the character of the righteousness that all who enter heaven will possess. Throughout the Sermon on the Mount He describes its fruits, and now in one sentence He points out its source and its nature: Be perfect as God is perfect. The law is but a transcript of the character of God. Behold in your heavenly Father a perfect manifestation of the principles which are the foundation of His government.

God is love. Like rays of light from the sun, love and light and joy flow out from Him to all His creatures. It is His nature to give. His very life is the outflow of unselfish love.

"His glory is His children's good;
His joy, His tender Fatherhood."

He tells us to be perfect as He is, in the same manner. We are to be centers of light and blessing to our little circle, even as He is to the universe. We have nothing of ourselves, but the light of His love shines upon us, and we are to reflect its brightness. "In His borrowed goodness good," we may be perfect in our sphere, even as God is perfect in His.

Jesus said, Be perfect as *your Father* is perfect. If you are the children of God you are partakers of His nature, and you can only be like Him. If you are God's children, begotten by His Spirit, you live by the life of God. In Christ dwells "all the fullness of the Godhead bodily" (Colossians 2:9). The life of Jesus is made manifest "in our mortal flesh" (2 Corinthians 4:11). That life in you will produce the same character and manifest the same works as it did in Him. Thus you will be in harmony with every precept of His law, for "the law of the Lord is perfect, converting the soul" (Psalm 19:7). Through love "the righteous requirement of the law" will be "fulfilled in us who do not walk according to the flesh but according to the Spirit" (Romans 8:4).

The True Motive in Service

"Take heed that you do not do your charitable deeds before men, to be seen by them." Matthew 6:1.

The words of Christ on the mount were an expression of that which had been the unspoken teaching of His life, but which the people had failed to comprehend. They could not understand how, having such great power, He neglected to use it in securing what they regarded as the chief good. Their spirit and motives and methods were the opposite of His. While they claimed to be very jealous for the honor of the law, self-glory was the real object which they sought. Christ would make it manifest to them that the lover of self is a transgressor of the law.

In the days of Christ the Pharisees were continually trying to earn the favor of Heaven in order to secure the worldly honor and prosperity which they regarded as the reward of virtue. At the same time they paraded their acts of charity before the people in order to attract attention and gain a reputation for sanctity.

It is through the Holy Spirit that every good work is accomplished, and the Spirit is given to glorify, not the receiver, but the Giver.

Jesus rebuked their ostentation, declaring that God does not recognize such service and that the flattery and admiration of the people, which they so eagerly sought, was the only reward they would ever receive.

"When you do a charitable deed," He said, "do not let your left hand know what your right hand is doing, that your charitable deed may be in secret; and your Father who sees in secret will Himself reward you openly" (Matthew 6:3, 4).

In these words Jesus did not teach that acts of kindness should always be kept secret. Paul the apostle, writing by the Holy Spirit, did not conceal the generous self-sacrifice of the Macedonian Christians, but told of the grace that Christ had wrought in them, and thus others were imbued with the same spirit. He also wrote to the church at Corinth and said, "Your zeal has stirred up the majority" (2 Corinthians 9:2).

Christ's own words make His meaning plain, that in acts of charity the aim should not be to secure praise and honor from others. Real godliness never prompts an effort at display. Those who desire words of praise and flattery, and feed on them as a sweet morsel, are Christians in name only.

By their good works, Christ's followers are to bring glory, not to themselves, but to Him through whose grace and power they have wrought. It is through the Holy Spirit that every good work is accomplished, and the Spirit is given to glorify, not the receiver, but the Giver. When the light of Christ is shining in the soul, the lips will be filled with praise and thanksgiving to God. Jesus will be magnified, self will be hidden, and Christ will appear as all in all.

We are not to think of reward, but of service. Yet kindness shown in this spirit will not fail of its recompense. "Your Father who sees in secret will Himself reward you." While it is true that God Himself is the great Reward that embraces every other, the soul receives and enjoys Him only as it becomes assimilated to Him in character. As we give ourselves to God for service, He gives Himself to us.

All who give place in their hearts and lives for the stream of God's blessing to flow to others will receive in themselves a rich reward. The hillsides and plains that furnish a channel for the mountain streams to reach the sea suffer no loss thereby. That which they give is repaid a hundredfold. For the stream that goes singing on its way leaves behind its gift of verdure and fruitfulness. The grass on its banks is a fresher green, the trees have a richer verdure, the flowers are more abundant. When the earth lies bare and brown under the summer's parching heat, a line of verdure marks the river's course, a witness to the recompense that God's grace imparts to all who give themselves as a channel for its outflow to the world.

This is the blessing of those who show mercy to the poor. While those who give to the needy bless others, they themselves are blessed in a still greater degree. The grace of Christ in the soul is developing traits of character that are the opposite of selfishness—traits that will refine, ennoble, and enrich the life. Acts of kindness performed in secret will bind hearts together and will draw them closer to the heart of Him from whom every generous impulse springs. The little attentions, the small acts of love and self-sacrifice, that flow out from the life as quietly as the fragrance from a flower—these constitute no small share of the blessings and happiness of life. And it will be found at last that the denial of self for the good and happiness of others, however humble and uncommended here, is recognized in heaven as the token of our union with Him, the King of glory, who was rich, yet for our sake became poor.

The deeds of kindness may have been done in secret, but the result upon the character of the doer cannot be hidden. Those who have sought for the development and perfection of Christian character by exercising these faculties in good works will, in the world to come, reap that which they have sown.

"When you pray, you shall not be like the hypocrites." Matthew 6:5.

The Pharisees had stated hours for prayer, and when they were abroad at the appointed time, they would pause wherever they might be—perhaps in the street or the marketplace, amid the hurrying throngs—and there in a loud voice rehearse their formal prayers. Such worship, offered merely for self-glorification, called forth unsparing rebuke from Jesus. He did not, however, discountenance public prayer, for He Himself prayed with His disciples and in the presence of the multitude. But He teaches that private prayer is not to be made public. In secret devotion our prayers are to reach the ears of none but the prayer-hearing God.

"When you pray, go into your room, and when you have shut the door, pray to your Father who is in the secret place" (verse 6). Have a place for secret prayer. Jesus had select places for communion with God, and so should we. We need often to retire to some spot, however humble, where we can be alone with God.

"Pray to your Father who is in the secret place." In the name of Jesus we may come into God's presence with the confidence of a child. No human being is needed to act as a mediator. Through Jesus we may open our hearts to God as to one who knows and loves us.

In the secret place of prayer, where no eye but God's can see, no ear but His can hear, we may pour out our most hidden desires and longings to the Father of infinite pity, and in the hush and silence of the soul that voice which never fails to answer the cry of human need will speak to our hearts.

Those who seek God in secret, telling the Lord their needs and pleading for help, will not plead in vain. As we make Christ our daily companion we shall feel that the powers of an unseen world are all around us. By looking to Jesus we shall become assimilated to His image. By beholding we become changed. The character is softened, refined, and ennobled for the heavenly kingdom. The sure result of communion and fellowship with our Lord will be to increase piety, purity, and fervor. We are receiving a divine education, and this is illustrated in a life of diligence and zeal.

The soul that turns to God for help, support, power, by daily, earnest prayer will have noble aspirations, clear perceptions of truth and duty, lofty purposes of action, and a continual hungering and thirsting after righteousness. By maintaining a connection with God, we shall be enabled to diffuse to others, through our association with them, the light, the peace, the serenity, that rule in our hearts. The strength acquired in prayer to God, united with persevering effort in training the mind in thoughtfulness and caretaking, prepares one for daily duties and keeps the spirit in peace under all circumstances.

If we draw near to God, He will put a word in our mouth to speak for Him, even praise for His name. He will teach us a strain from the song of the angels, even thanksgiving to our heavenly Father. In every act of life, the light and love of an indwelling Savior will be revealed. Outward troubles cannot reach the life that is lived by faith in the Son of God.

"When you pray, do not use vain repetitions as the heathen do."
Matthew 6:7.

The heathen looked upon their prayers as having in themselves merit to atone for sin. Hence the longer the prayer the greater the merit. If they could become holy by their own efforts they would have some ground for boasting. This idea of prayer is an outworking of the principle of self-expiation which lies at the foundation of all systems of false religion. The Pharisees had adopted this pagan idea of prayer, and it is by no means extinct in our day, even among those who profess to be Christians. The repetition of set, customary phrases, when the heart feels no need of God, is of the same character as the "vain repetitions" of pagans.

Prayer is not an expiation for sin. It has no virtue or merit of itself.

43

All the flowery words at our command are not equivalent to one holy desire. The most eloquent prayers are but idle words if they do not express the true sentiments of the heart. But the prayer that comes from an earnest heart, when the simple wants of the soul are expressed, as we would ask an earthly friend for a favor, expecting it to be granted—this is the prayer of faith. God does not desire our ceremonial compliments, but the unspoken cry of the heart broken and subdued with a sense of its sin and utter weakness finds its way to the Father of all mercy.

"When you fast, do not be like the hypocrites." Matthew 6:16.

The fasting which the Word of God enjoins is something more than a form. It does not consist merely in refusing food, in wearing sackcloth, in sprinkling ashes upon the head. A person who fasts in real sorrow for sin will never court display.

The object of the fast which God calls upon us to keep is not to afflict the body for the sin of the soul, but to aid us in perceiving the grievous character of sin, in humbling the heart before God and receiving His pardoning grace. His command to Israel was "Rend your heart, and not your garments; return to the Lord your God" (Joel 2:13).

It will avail nothing for us to do penance or to flatter ourselves that by our own works we shall merit or purchase an inheritance among the saints. When the question was asked Christ, "What shall we do, that we may work the works of God?" He answered, "This is the work of God, that you believe in Him whom He sent" (John 6:28, 29). Repentance is turning from self to Christ, and when we receive Christ so that through faith He can live His life in us, good works will be manifest.

Jesus said, "When you fast, anoint your head and wash your face, so that you do not appear to men to be fasting, but to your Father who is in the secret place" (Matthew 6:17, 18). Whatever is done to the glory of God is to be done with cheerfulness, not with sadness and gloom. There is nothing gloomy in the religion of Jesus. If Christians give the impression by a mournful attitude that they have been disappointed in their Lord, they misrepresent His character and put arguments into the mouth of His enemies. Though in words they may claim God as their Father, yet in gloom and sorrow they present to the world the aspect of spiritual orphans.

Christ desires us to make His service appear attractive, as it really is.

44

Let the self-denials and the secret heart trials be revealed only to the compassionate Savior. Let the burdens be left at the foot of the cross, and go on your way rejoicing in His love who first loved you. Other people may never know of the work going on secretly between the soul and God, but the result of the Spirit's work upon the heart will be manifest to all, for He "who sees in secret will reward you openly" (verse 18).

"Do not lay up for yourselves treasures on earth." Matthew 6:19.

Treasure laid up on earth will not endure. Thieves break through and steal. Moth and rust corrupt. Fire and storm sweep away your possessions. And "where your treasure is, there your heart will be also" (verse 21). Treasure laid up on the earth will engross the mind to the exclusion of heavenly things.

The instruction is to lay up treasures in heaven for yourselves. It is for your own interest to secure heavenly riches. These alone, of all that you possess, are really yours. The treasure laid up in heaven is imperishable. No fire or flood can destroy it, no thief despoil it, no moth or rust corrupt it. It is in the keeping of God.

This treasure, which Christ esteems as precious above all estimate, is "the riches of the glory of His inheritance in the saints" (Ephesians 1:18). The disciples of Christ are called His jewels, His precious and peculiar treasure. He says that they will be "like the jewels of a crown" (Zechariah 9:16). Christ looks upon His people in their purity and perfection as the reward of all His sufferings, His humiliation, and His love, and the supplement of His glory.

Character is the great harvest of life. And every word or deed that through the grace of Christ shall kindle in one soul an impulse that reaches heavenward, every effort that tends to the formation of a Christlike character, is laying up treasure in heaven.

Where the treasure is, there the heart will be. In every effort to benefit others, we benefit ourselves. And at the final day, when the wealth of earth shall perish, those who have laid up treasure in heaven will behold that which their lives have gained.

"If then you were raised with Christ, seek those things which are above, where Christ is, sitting at the right hand of God" (Colossians 3:1).

"If therefore your eye is good, your whole body will be full of light."
Matthew 6:22.

Singleness of purpose, wholehearted devotion to God, is the condition pointed out by the Savior's words. Let the purpose be sincere and unwavering to discern the truth and to obey it at whatever cost, and you will receive divine enlightenment. Real piety begins when all compromise with sin is at an end. Then the language of the heart will be that of the apostle Paul: "One thing I do, forgetting those things which are behind and reaching forward to those things which are ahead, I press toward the goal for the prize of the upward call of God in Christ Jesus" (Philippians 3:13, 14). "I also count all things loss for the excellence of the knowledge of Christ Jesus my Lord, for whom I have suffered the loss of all things, and count them as rubbish" (verse 8).

But when the eye is blinded by the love of self, there is only darkness. "If your eye is bad, your whole body will be full of darkness" (Matthew 6:23). Yielding to temptation begins in permitting the mind to waver, to be inconstant in your trust in God. If we do not choose to give ourselves fully to God, then we are in darkness. When we make any reserve, we are leaving open a door through which Satan can enter to lead us astray by his temptations. He knows that if he can obscure our vision, so that the eye of faith cannot see God, there will be no barrier against sin.

The prevalence of a sinful desire shows the delusion of the soul. Every indulgence of that desire strengthens the soul's aversion to God. In following the path of Satan's choosing, we are encompassed by the shadows of evil, and every step leads into deeper darkness and increases the blindness of the heart.

The same law obtains in the spiritual as in the natural world. Those who abide in darkness will at last lose the power of vision. They will be shut in by a deeper than midnight blackness. To them the brightest noontide can bring no light. Through persistently cherishing evil, willfully disregarding the pleadings of divine love, sinners lose the love for good, the desire for God, the very capacity to receive the light of heaven. The invitation of mercy is still full of love, the light is shining as brightly as when it first dawned upon the soul, but the voice falls on deaf ears, the light on blinded eyes.

Our heavenly Father follows us with appeals and warnings and assurances of compassion, until further opportunities and privileges would be wholly in vain. The responsibility rests with us as sinners. By resisting the Spirit of God today, we prepare the way for a second resistance of light when it comes with mightier power. Thus we pass on from one stage of resistance to another, until at last the light will fail to impress, and we will cease to respond in any measure to the Spirit of God.

"No one can serve two masters." Matthew 6:24.

Christ does not say that men and women will not or shall not serve two masters, but that they *cannot*. The interests of God and the interests of mammon have no union or sympathy. Just where the conscience of Christians warns them to forbear, to deny themselves, to stop, just there worldlings step over the line, to indulge their selfish propensities. On one side of the line are the self-denying followers of Christ. On the other side are the self-indulgent world lovers, pandering to fashion, engaging in frivolity, and pampering themselves in forbidden pleasure.

No one can occupy a neutral position. There is no middle class, who neither love God nor serve the enemy of righteousness. Christ is to live in His human agents and work through their faculties and act through their capabilities. Their will must be submitted to His will. They must act with His Spirit. Then it is no more they that live, but Christ that lives in them. Those who do not give themselves wholly to God are under the control of another power, listening to another voice, whose suggestions are of an entirely different character. Half-and-half service places the human agent on the side of the enemy as an ally of the hosts of darkness. When those who claim to be soldiers of Christ engage with the confederacy of Satan, and help along his side, they prove themselves enemies of Christ. They betray sacred trusts. They form a link between Satan and the true soldiers, so that through these agencies the enemy is constantly working to steal away the hearts of Christ's soldiers.

The strongest bulwark of vice in our world is not the iniquitous life of the abandoned sinner or the degraded outcast. It is that life which otherwise appears virtuous, honorable, and noble, but in which one sin is fostered, one vice indulged. To the soul that is struggling in secret against some giant temptation, trembling upon the very verge of the precipice, such an example is one of the most powerful enticements to sin. Any person who, endowed with high conceptions of life and truth and honor, yet willfully transgresses one precept of God's holy law, has perverted His noble gifts into a lure to sin. Genius, talent, sympathy, even generous and kindly deeds, may become decoys of Satan to entice other souls over the precipice of ruin for this life and the life to come.

"Do not love the world or the things in the world. If anyone loves the world, the love of the Father is not in him. For all that is in the world—the lust of the flesh, the lust of the eyes, and the pride of of life—is not of the Father but is of the world" (1 John 2:15, 16).

"Do not worry about your life." Matthew 6:25.

He who has given you life knows your need of food to sustain it. He who created the body is not unmindful of your need for clothing. Will not He who has bestowed the greater gift bestow also what is needed to make it complete?

Jesus pointed His hearers to the birds as they warbled their carols of praise, unencumbered with thoughts of care, for "they neither sow nor reap" (verse 26), yet the great Father provides for their needs. And He asks, "Are you not of more value than they?"

> "No sparrow falls without His care,
>   No soul bows low but Jesus knows;
>   For He is with us everywhere,
>   And marks each bitter tear that flows.
>   And He will never, never, never
>   Forsake the soul that trusts Him ever."

The hillsides and the fields were bright with flowers, and, pointing to them in the dewy freshness of the morning, Jesus said, "Consider the lilies of the field, how they grow" (verse 28). The graceful forms and delicate hues of the plants and flowers may be copied by human skill, but what touch can impart life to even one flower or blade of grass? Every wayside blossom owes its being to the same power that set the starry worlds on high. Through all created things thrills one pulse of life from the great heart of God. The flowers of the field are clothed by His hand in richer robes than have ever graced the forms of earthly kings. And "if God so clothes the grass of the field, which today is, and tomorrow is thrown into the oven, will He not much more clothe you, O you of little faith?" (verse 30).

It is He who made the flowers and who gave to the sparrow its song who says, "Consider the lilies," "Look at the birds." In the loveliness of the things of nature you may learn more of the wisdom of God than even highly educated people know. On the lily's petals God has written a message for you, written in language that your heart can read only as it unlearns the lessons of distrust and selfishness and corroding care.

Why has He given you the singing birds and the gentle blossoms, but from the overflowing love of a Father's heart, that would brighten and gladden your path of life? All that was needed for existence would have been yours without the flowers and birds, but God was not content to provide what would suffice for mere existence. He has filled earth and air and sky with glimpses of beauty to tell you of His loving thought for you. If He has lavished such infinite skill upon the things of nature for your happiness and joy, can you doubt that He will give you every needed blessing?

"Consider the lilies." Through the flowers God would call our attention to the loveliness of Christlike character. He who has given such beauty to the blossoms desires far more that the soul should be clothed with the beauty of the character of Christ.

Consider, says Jesus, how the lilies grow. Springing from the cold, dark earth, or from the mud of the riverbed, the plants unfold in loveliness and fragrance. Who would dream of the possibilities of beauty in the rough brown bulb of the lily? But when the life of God, hidden therein, unfolds at His call in the rain and the sunshine, human beings marvel at the vision of grace and loveliness. Even so will the life of God unfold in every human soul that will yield itself to the ministry of His grace, which, free as the rain and the sunshine, comes with its benediction to all. It is the Word of God that creates the flowers, and the same Word will produce in you the graces of His Spirit.

God's law is the law of love. He has surrounded you with beauty to teach you that you are not placed on earth merely to dig and build, to toil and spin, but to make life bright and joyous and beautiful with the love of Christ—like the flowers, to gladden other lives by the ministry of love.

Fathers and mothers, let your children learn from the flowers. Take them with you into garden and field and under the leafy trees, and teach them to read in nature the message of God's love.

Teach the children that because of God's great love their natures may be changed and brought into harmony with His. Teach them, as they gather the sweet blossoms, that He who made the flowers is more beautiful than they. Thus the tendrils of their hearts will be entwined about Him who is "altogether lovely." He will become to them as a daily companion and familiar friend, and their lives will be transformed into the image of His purity.

"Seek first the kingdom of God." Matthew 6:33.

The people who listened to the words of Christ were still anxiously watching for some announcement of the earthly kingdom. While Jesus was opening to them the treasures of heaven, the question uppermost in many minds was How will a connection with Him advance our prospects in the world? Jesus shows that in making the things of the world their supreme anxiety they were

If you give yourself to God's service, He who has all power in heaven and earth will provide for your needs.

like the nations about them, living as if there were no God, whose tender care is over His creatures.

"All these things the nations of the world seek after," said Jesus, "and your Father knows that you need these things. But seek the kingdom of God, and all these things shall be added to you" (Luke 12:30). I have come to open to you the kingdom of love and righteousness and peace. Open your hearts to receive this kingdom, and make its service your highest interest. Though it is a spiritual kingdom, fear not that your needs for this life will be uncared-for. If you give yourself to God's service, He who has all power in heaven and earth will provide for your needs.

Jesus does not release us from the necessity of effort, but He teaches that we are to make Him first and last and best in everything. We are to engage in no business, follow no pursuit, seek no pleasure, that would hinder the outworking of His righteousness in our character and life.

Jesus, while on earth, dignified life in all its details by keeping before men and women the glory of God, and by subordinating everything to the will of His Father. If we follow His example, His assurance to us is that all things needful in this life "shall be added" (Matthew 6:33).

God's everlasting arm encircles the soul that turns to Him for aid, however feeble that soul may be. The precious things of the hills shall perish, but the soul that lives for God shall abide with Him. "The world is passing away, and the lust of it; but he who does the will of God abides forever" (1 John 2:17). The city of God will open its golden gates to receive those who learned while on earth to lean on God for guidance and wisdom, for comfort and hope, amid loss and affliction.

"Do not worry about tomorrow, for tomorrow will worry about its own things. Sufficient for the day is its own trouble." Matthew 6:34.

If you have given yourself to God, to do His work, you have no need to be anxious for tomorrow. He whose servant you are knows the end from the beginning. The events of tomorrow, which are hidden from your view, are open to the eyes of Him who is omnipotent.

When we take into our hands the management of things with which we have to do, and depend upon our own wisdom for success, we are taking a burden which God has not given us, and are trying to bear it without His aid. We are taking upon ourselves the responsibility that belongs to God, and thus are really putting ourselves in His place. We may well have anxiety and anticipate danger and loss, for it is certain to befall us. But when we really believe that God loves us and means to do us good, we shall cease to worry about the future. We shall trust God as a child trusts a loving parent. Then our troubles and torments will disappear, for our will is swallowed up in the will of God.

One day alone is ours, and during this day we are to live for God. For this one day we are to place in the hand of Christ, in solemn service, all our purposes and plans, casting all our care upon Him, for He cares for us. "I know the thoughts that I think toward you, says the Lord, thoughts of peace and not of evil, to give you a future and a hope" (Jeremiah 29:11). "In returning and rest you shall be saved; in quietness and confidence shall be your strength" (Isaiah 30:15).

If you will seek the Lord and be converted every day, if you will come wearing the yoke of Christ—the yoke of obedience and service—all your murmurings will be stilled, all the perplexing problems that now confront you will be solved.

The Lord's Prayer

"In this manner, therefore pray." Matthew 6:9.

The Lord's Prayer was given twice by our Savior, first to the multitude in the Sermon on the Mount, and again, some months later, to the disciples alone. The disciples had been for a short time absent from their Lord, when on their return they found Him absorbed in communion with God. Seeming unconscious of their presence, He continued praying aloud. The Savior's face was irradiated with a celestial brightness. He seemed to be in the very presence of the Unseen, and there was a living power in His words as of one who spoke with God.

The hearts of the listening disciples were deeply moved. They had noticed how often He spent long hours in solitude in communion with His Father. His days were passed in ministry to the crowds that pressed upon Him and in unveiling the treacherous sophistry of the rabbis, and this incessant labor often left Him so utterly wearied that His mother and brothers, and even His disciples, had feared that His life would be sacrificed. But as He returned from the hours of prayer that closed the toilsome day, they marked the look of peace upon His face, the sense of refreshment that seemed to pervade His presence. It was from hours spent with God that He came forth, morning by morning, to bring the light of heaven to humanity.

The disciples had come to connect His hours of prayer with the power of His words and works. Now, as they listened to His supplication, their hearts were awed and humbled. As He ceased praying, it was with a conviction of their own deep need that they exclaimed, "Lord, teach us to pray" (Luke 11:1).

Jesus gives them no new form of prayer. That which He has before taught them He repeats, as if He would say, You need to understand what I have already given. It has a depth of meaning you have not yet fathomed.

The Savior does not, however, restrict us to the use of these exact words. As one with humanity, He presents His own ideal of prayer, words so simple that they may be adopted by the little child, yet so comprehensive that their significance can never be fully grasped by the greatest minds. We are taught to come to God with our tribute of thanksgiving, to make known our wants, to confess our sins, and to claim His mercy in accordance with His promise.

"When you pray, say: Our Father." Luke 11:2.

Jesus teaches us to call *His* Father *our* Father. So ready, so eager, is the Savior's heart to welcome us as members of the family of God, that in the very first words we are to use in approaching God He places the assurance of our divine relationship: "Our Father."

Here is the announcement of that wonderful truth, so full of encouragement and comfort, that God loves us as He loves His Son. This is what Jesus said in His last prayer for His disciples: You "have loved them as You have loved Me" (John 17:23).

The world that Satan has claimed and has ruled over with cruel tyranny, the Son of God has, by one vast achievement, encircled in His love and connected again with the throne of Jehovah. Cherubim and seraphim, and the unnumbered hosts of all the unfallen worlds, sang anthems of praise to God and the Lamb when this triumph was assured. They rejoiced that the way of salvation had been opened to the fallen race and that the earth would be redeemed from the curse of sin. How much more should those rejoice who are the objects of such amazing love!

How can we ever be in doubt and uncertainty, and feel that we are orphans? It was in behalf of those who had transgressed the law that Jesus took upon Him human nature. He became like us, that we might have everlasting peace and assurance. We have an Advocate in the heavens. Whoever accepts Him as a personal Savior is not left an orphan to bear the burden of his or her own sins.

"Beloved, now we are children of God" (1 John 3:2). "And if children, then heirs—heirs of God and joint heirs with Christ; if indeed we suffer with Him, that we may also be glorified together" (Romans 8:17).

The very first step in approaching God is to know and believe the love that He has for us (1 John 4:16), for it is through the drawing of His love that we are led to come to Him.

The perception of God's love works the renunciation of selfishness. In calling God our Father, we recognize all His children as our brothers and sisters. We are all a part of the great web of humanity, all members of one family. In our petitions we are to include our neighbors as well as ourselves. No one prays aright who seeks a blessing for self alone.

He cares for our necessities, and His love and mercy and grace are continually flowing to satisfy our need.

The infinite God, said Jesus, makes it your privilege to approach Him by the name of Father. Understand all that this implies. No earthly parent ever pleaded so earnestly with an erring child as He who made you pleads with the transgressor. He hears every word that is spoken, listens to every prayer that is offered, tastes the sorrows and disappointments of every soul, regards the treatment that is given to father, mother, sister, friend, and neighbor. He cares for our necessities, and His love and mercy and grace are continually flowing to satisfy our need.

But if you call God your Father you acknowledge yourselves His children, to be guided by His wisdom and to be obedient in all things, knowing that His love is changeless. You will accept His plan for your life. As children of God, you will hold His honor, His character, His family, His work, as the objects of your highest interest. It will be your joy to recognize and honor your relation to your Father and to every member of His family. You will rejoice to do any act, however humble, that will tend to His glory or to the well-being of your kindred.

"Our God is in heaven; He does whatever He pleases" (Psalm 115:3). In His care we may safely rest, saying, "Whenever I am afraid, I will trust in You" (Psalm 56:3).

"Hallowed be Your name." Matthew 6:9.

To hallow the name of the Lord requires that the words in which we speak of the Supreme Being be uttered with reverence. "Holy and awesome is His name" (Psalm 111:9). We are never in any manner to treat lightly the titles or appellations of the Deity. In prayer we enter the audience chamber of the Most High. We should come before Him with holy awe. The angels veil their faces in His presence. The cherubim and the bright and holy seraphim approach His throne with solemn reverence. How much more should we, finite, sinful beings, come in a reverent manner before the Lord, our Maker!

But to hallow the name of the Lord means much more than this. "The name of the Lord" is "merciful and gracious, longsuffering, and abounding in goodness and truth, . . . forgiving iniquity and transgression and sin" (Exodus 34:5-7). Of the church of Christ it is written, "This is the name by which she will be called: THE LORD OUR RIGHTEOUSNESS" (Jeremiah 33:16). This name is put upon every follower of Christ. The prophet Jeremiah, in the time of Israel's sore distress and tribulation, prayed, "We are called by Your name; do not leave us!" (Jeremiah 14:9).

This name is hallowed by the angels of heaven, by the inhabitants of unfallen worlds. When you pray, "Hallowed be Your name," you ask that it may be hallowed in this world, hallowed in you. God has acknowledged you before human beings and angels as His child. Pray that you may do no dishonor to the "noble name by which you are called" (James 2:7). God sends you into the world as His representative. In every act of life you are to make manifest the name of God.

This petition calls upon you to possess His character. You cannot hallow His name, you cannot represent Him to the world, unless in life and character you represent the very life and character of God. This you can do only through the acceptance of the grace and righteousness of Christ.

"Your kingdom come." Matthew 6:10.

God is our Father, who loves and cares for us as His children. He is also the great King of the universe. The interests of His kingdom are our interests, and we are to work for its upbuilding.

The disciples of Christ were looking for the immediate coming of the kingdom of His glory, but in giving them this prayer Jesus taught that the kingdom was not then to be established. They were to pray for its coming as an event yet future. But this petition was also an assurance to them. While they were not to behold the coming of the kingdom in their day, the fact that Jesus bade them pray for it is evidence that in God's own time it will surely come.

The kingdom of God's grace is now being established, as day by day hearts that have been full of sin and rebellion yield to the sovereignty of His love. But the full establishment of the kingdom of His glory will not take place until the second coming of Christ to this world. "The kingdom and dominion, and the greatness of the kingdoms under the whole heaven" is to be given to "the people, the saints of the Most High" (Daniel 7:27). And Christ will take to Himself His great power and will reign.

*T*he heavenly gates are again to be lifted up, and with ten thousand times ten thousand and thousands of thousands of holy ones, our Savior will come forth as King of kings and Lord of lords. Jehovah Immanuel "shall be King over all the earth" (Zechariah 14:9). "The tabernacle of God" shall be with the human race, "and He will dwell with them, and they shall be His people, and God Himself will be with them and be their God" (Revelation 21:3).

But before that coming, Jesus said, "This gospel of the kingdom will be preached in all the world as a witness to all the nations" (Matthew 24:14). His kingdom will not come until the good tidings of His grace have been carried to all the earth. Hence, as we give ourselves to God, and win other souls to Him, we hasten the coming of His kingdom. Only those who devote themselves to His service, saying, "Here am I! Send me" (Isaiah 6:8)—they alone pray in sincerity, "Your kingdom come."

"Your will be done on earth as it is in heaven." Matthew 6:10.

The will of God is expressed in the precepts of His holy law, and the principles of this law are the principles of heaven. The angels of heaven attain no higher knowledge than to know the will of God, and to do His will is the highest service that can engage their powers.

But in heaven, service is not rendered in the spirit of legality. When Satan rebelled against the law of Jehovah, the thought that there was a law came to the angels almost as an awakening to something unthought-of. In their ministry the angels are not as servants, but as sons. There is perfect unity between them and their Creator. Obedience is to them no drudgery. Love for God makes their service a joy. So in every soul wherein Christ, the hope of glory, dwells, His words are reechoed: "I delight to do Your will, O my God, and Your law is within my heart" (Psalm 40:8).

The petition "Your will be done on earth as it is in heaven" is a prayer that the reign of evil on this earth may be ended, that sin may be forever destroyed, and the kingdom of righteousness be established. Then in earth as in heaven will be fulfilled "all the good pleasure of His goodness" (2 Thessalonians 1:11).

"Give us this day our daily bread." Matthew 6:11.

The first half of the prayer Jesus has taught us is in regard to the name and kingdom and will of God—that His name may be honored, His kingdom established, His will performed. When you have thus made God's service your first interest, you may ask with confidence that your own needs may be supplied. If you have renounced self and given yourself to Christ you are a member of the family of God. Everything in the Father's house is for you. The ministry of angels, the gift of His Spirit, the labors of His servants—all are for you. The world, with everything in it, is yours so far as it can do you good. Even the enmity of the wicked will prove a blessing by disciplining you for heaven. If "you are Christ's" (1 Corinthians 3:23), "all things are yours" (verse 21).

But you are as a child who is not yet placed in control of his inheritance. God does not entrust to you your precious possession, lest Satan by his wily arts should beguile you, as he did the first pair in Eden. Christ holds it for you, safe beyond the spoiler's reach. Like the child, you shall receive day by day what is required for the day's need. Every day you are to pray, "Give us this day our daily bread." Be not dismayed if you have not sufficient for tomorrow. That God who sent the ravens to feed Elijah by the brook Cherith will not pass by one of His faithful, self-sacrificing children. Of all who walk righteously it is written: "They shall not be ashamed in the evil time, and in the days of famine they shall be satisfied" (Psalm 37:19). "He who did not spare His own Son, but delivered Him up for us all, how shall He not with Him also freely give us all things?" (Romans 8:32).

He who lightened the cares and anxieties of His widowed mother and helped her to provide for the household at Nazareth sympathizes with every mother in her struggle to provide her children food. He who had compassion on the multitude because they "were weary and scattered like sheep" (Matthew 9:36) still has compassion on the suffering poor.

When we pray, "Give us this day our daily bread," we ask for others as well as ourselves. And we acknowledge that what God gives us is not for ourselves alone. God gives to us in trust, that we may feed the hungry. Of His goodness He has prepared for the poor (Psalm 68:10). And He says, "When you give a dinner or a supper, do not ask your friends, your brothers, your relatives, nor your rich neighbors. . . . But when you give a feast, invite the poor, the maimed, the lame, the blind. And you will be blessed, because they cannot repay you; for you shall be repaid at the resurrection of the just" (Luke 14:12-14).

The prayer for daily bread includes not only food to sustain the body, but that spiritual bread which will nourish the soul for everlasting life. Jesus bids us, "Do not labor for the food which perishes, but for the food which endures to everlasting life" (John 6:27). He says, "I am the living bread which came down from heaven. If anyone eats of this bread, he will live forever" (verse 51). Our Savior is the bread of life, and it is by beholding His love, by receiving it into the soul, that we feed upon the bread which came down from heaven.

We receive Christ through His Word, and the Holy Spirit is given to open the Word of God to our understanding and bring home its truths to our hearts. We are to pray day by day that as we read His Word, God will send His Spirit to reveal to us the truth that will strengthen our souls for the day's need.

In teaching us to ask every day for what we need—both temporal and spiritual blessings—God has a purpose to accomplish for our good. He would have us realize our dependence upon His constant care, for He is seeking to draw us into communion with Himself. In this communion, through prayer and study of the precious truths of His Word, we shall be fed. We shall be refreshed at the fountain of life.

"Forgive us our sins, for we also forgive everyone who is indebted to us."
Luke 11:4.

Jesus teaches that we can receive forgiveness from God only as we forgive others. It is the love of God that draws us to Him, and that love cannot touch our hearts without creating love for others.

After completing the Lord's Prayer, Jesus added: "If you forgive men their trespasses, your heavenly Father will also forgive you. But if you do not forgive men their trespasses, neither will your Father forgive your trespasses" (Matthew 6:14, 15). Those who are unforgiving cut off the very channel through which alone they can receive mercy from God.

We should not think that unless those who have injured us confess the wrong we are justified in withholding from them our forgiveness. It is their part, no doubt, to humble their hearts by repentance and confession. But we are to have a spirit of compassion toward those who have trespassed against us, whether or not they confess their faults. However sorely they may have wounded us, we are not to cherish our grievances, but as we hope to be pardoned for our offenses against God we are to pardon all who have done evil to us.

But forgiveness has a broader meaning than many suppose. When God gives the promise that He "will abundantly pardon" (Isaiah 55:7), He adds, as if the meaning of that promise exceeded all that we could comprehend: "'My thoughts are not your thoughts, nor are your ways My ways.' . . . 'For as the heavens are higher than the earth, so are My ways higher than your ways, and My thoughts than your thoughts'" (verses 8, 9). God's forgiveness is not merely a judicial act by which He sets us free from condemnation. It is not only forgiveness *for* sin, but reclaiming *from* sin. It is the outflow of redeeming love that transforms the heart. David had the true conception of forgiveness when he prayed, "Create in me a clean heart, O God, and renew a steadfast spirit within me" (Psalm 51:10).

God in Christ gave Himself for our sins. He suffered the cruel death of the cross, bore for us the burden of guilt, "the just for the unjust," that He might reveal to us His love and draw us to Himself. And He says, "Be kind to one another, tenderhearted, forgiving one another, even as God in Christ forgave you" (Ephesians 4:32). Let Christ, the divine Life, dwell in you and through you reveal the heaven-born love that will inspire hope in the hopeless and bring heaven's peace to the sin-stricken heart.

The one thing essential for us in order that we may receive and impart the forgiving love of God is to know and believe the love that He has to us (1 John 4:16). Satan is working by every deception he can command, in order that we may not discern that love. He will lead us to think that our mistakes and transgressions have been so grievous that the Lord will reject our prayers and will not bless and save us. But we may tell the enemy that "the blood of Jesus Christ His Son cleanses us from all sin" (1 John 1:7).

When we feel that we have sinned and cannot pray, it is then the time to pray. Ashamed we may be and deeply humbled, but we must pray and believe. Forgiveness, reconciliation with God, does not come to us as a reward for our works. It is not bestowed because of the merit of sinful human beings, but is a gift.

We should not try to lessen our guilt by excusing sin. We must accept God's estimate of sin, and that is heavy indeed. Calvary alone can reveal the terrible enormity of sin. If we had to bear our own guilt, it would crush us. But the sinless One has taken our place. He has borne our iniquity. "If we confess our sins," God "is faithful and just to forgive us our sins and to cleanse us from all unrighteousness" (verse 9). Glorious truth!

> *Every temptation resisted, every trial bravely borne, gives us a new experience and advances us in the work of character building.*

"Do not lead us into temptation, but deliver us from the evil one." Matthew 6:13.

Temptation is enticement to sin, and this does not proceed from God, but from Satan and from the evil of our own hearts. "God cannot be tempted by evil, nor does He Himself tempt anyone" (James 1:13).

Satan seeks to bring us into temptation, that the evil of our characters may be revealed before both humans and angels, that he may claim us as his own. In the symbolic prophecy of Zechariah, Satan is seen standing at the right hand of the Angel of the Lord, accusing Joshua, the high priest, who is clothed in filthy garments and resisting the work that the Angel desires to do for him. This represents the attitude of Satan toward every soul whom Christ is seeking to draw to Himself. The enemy leads us into sin, then accuses us before the heavenly universe as unworthy of the love of God. But "the Lord said to Satan, 'The Lord rebuke you, Satan! The Lord who has chosen Jerusalem rebuke you! Is this not a brand plucked from the fire?'" (Zechariah 3:2). And to Joshua He said, "See, I have removed your iniquity from you, and I will clothe you with rich robes" (verse 4).

God in His great love is seeking to develop in us the precious graces of His Spirit. He permits us to encounter obstacles, persecution, and hardships, not as a curse but as the greatest blessing of our lives. Every temptation resisted, every trial bravely borne, gives us a new experience and advances us in the work of character building. The soul that through divine power resists temptation reveals to the world and to the heavenly universe the efficiency of the grace of Christ.

But while we are not to be dismayed by trial, bitter though it be, we should pray that God will not permit us to be brought where we shall be drawn away by the desires of our own evil hearts. In offering the prayer that Christ has given, we surrender ourselves to the guidance of God, asking Him to lead us in safe paths. We cannot offer this prayer in sincerity and yet decide to walk in any way of our own choosing. We shall wait for His hand to lead us; we shall listen to His voice, saying, "This is the way, walk in it" (Isaiah 30:21).

It is not safe for us to linger to contemplate the advantages to be gained through yielding to Satan's suggestions. If we venture on Satan's ground we have no assurance of protection from his power. So far as in us lies, we should close every avenue by which the tempter may find access to us.

The prayer "Do not lead us into temptation" is itself a promise. If we commit ourselves to God we have the assurance, He "will not allow you to be tempted beyond what you are able, but with the temptation will also make the way of escape, that you may be able to bear it" (1 Corinthians 10:13).

The only safeguard against evil is the indwelling of Christ in the heart through faith in His righteousness. It is because selfishness exists in our hearts that temptation has power over us. But when we behold the great love of God, selfishness appears to us in its hideous and repulsive character, and we desire to have it expelled from the soul. As the Holy Spirit glorifies Christ, our hearts are softened and subdued, the temptation loses its power, and the grace of Christ transforms the character.

Christ will never abandon those for whom He has died. They may leave Him and be overwhelmed with temptation, but Christ can never turn from one for whom He has paid the ransom of His own life. Could our spiritual vision be strengthened, we should see souls bowed under oppression and burdened with grief, ready to die in discouragement. We should see angels flying swiftly to aid these tempted ones, who are standing as on the brink of a precipice. The angels from heaven force back the hosts of evil that encompass these souls, and guide them to plant their feet on the sure foundation.

Thank God, we are not left alone. He who "so loved the world that He gave His only begotten Son, that whoever believes in Him should not perish but have everlasting life" (John 3:16) will not desert us in the battle with the adversary of God and humanity.

Live in contact with the living Christ, and He will hold you firmly by a hand that will never let go. Know and believe the love that God has to us, and you are secure. That love is a fortress impregnable to all the delusions and assaults of Satan.

"Yours is the kingdom and the power and the glory." Matthew 6:13.

The last sentence of the Lord's Prayer, like the first, points to our Father as above all power and authority and every name that is named. The Savior beheld the years that stretched out before His disciples, not, as they had dreamed, lying in the sunshine of worldly prosperity and honor, but dark with the tempests of human hatred and satanic wrath. Amid national strife and ruin, the steps of the disciples would be beset with perils. Often their hearts would be oppressed by fear. They were to see Jerusalem a desolation, the Temple swept away, its worship forever ended, and Israel scattered to all lands.

Jesus said, "You will hear of wars and rumors of wars. . . . Nation will rise against nation, and kingdom against kingdom. And there will be famines, pestilences, and earthquakes in various places. All these are the beginning of sorrows" (Matthew 24:6-8). Yet Christ's followers were not to fear that their hope was lost or that God had forsaken the earth. The disciples of Christ were directed to look above all the power and dominion of evil to the Lord their God, whose kingdom rules over all and who is their Father and everlasting Friend.

The ruin of Jerusalem was a symbol of the final ruin that shall overwhelm the world. The prophecies that received a partial fulfillment in the overthrow of Jerusalem have a more direct application to the last days. We are now standing on the threshold of great and solemn events. A crisis is before us such as the world has never witnessed. And sweetly to us, as to the first disciples, comes the assurance that God's kingdom rules over all. The program of coming events is in the hands of our Maker. The Majesty of heaven has the destiny of nations, as well as the concerns of His church, in His own charge.

He who slumbers not, who is continually at work for the accomplishment of His designs, will carry forward His own work. He will thwart the purposes of wicked human beings and will bring to confusion the counsels of those who plot mischief against His people. He who is the King, the Lord of hosts, will amid the strife and tumult of nations guard His children still. He is our Savior, and His people will be safe in His hands.

Not Judging, but Doing

"Judge not, that you be not judged." Matthew 7:1.

The effort to earn salvation by one's own works inevitably leads men and women to pile up human exactions as a barrier against sin. Seeing that they fail to keep the law, they will devise rules and regulations of their own to force themselves to obey. All this turns the mind away from God to self. His love dies out of the heart, and with it perishes love for others. A system of human invention, with its multitudinous exactions, will lead its advocates to judge all who come short of the prescribed human standard. The atmosphere of selfish and narrow criticism stifles the noble and generous emotions, and causes people to become self-centered judges and petty spies.

The Pharisees were of this class. They came forth from their religious services, not humbled with a sense of their own weakness, not grateful for the great privileges that God had given them. Filled with spiritual pride, their theme was "Myself, my feelings, my knowledge, my ways." Their own attainments became the standard by which they judged others.

The people largely shared that same spirit, intruding upon the province of conscience and judging one another in matters that lay between the soul and God. It was in reference to this spirit and practice that Jesus said, "Judge not, that you be not judged." That is, do not set yourself up as a standard. Do not make your opinions, your views of duty, your interpretations of Scripture, a criterion for others and in your heart condemn them if they do not come up to your ideal. "Therefore judge nothing before the time, until the Lord comes, who will both bring to light the hidden things of darkness and reveal the counsels of the hearts" (1 Corinthians 4:5). We cannot read the heart. Ourselves faulty, we are not qualified to sit in judgment upon others. Finite human beings can judge only from outward appearance. To Him alone who knows the secret springs of action, and who deals tenderly and compassionately, is it given to decide the case of every soul.

"Therefore you are inexcusable, . . . whoever you are who judge, for in whatever you judge another you condemn yourself; for you who judge practice the same things" (Romans 2:1). Thus those who condemn or criticize others proclaim themselves guilty, for they do the same things. In condemning others, they are passing sentence upon themselves, and God declares that this sentence is just. He accepts their own verdict against themselves.

> *"Why do you look at the speck in your brother's eye,*
> *but do not consider the plank in your own eye?" Matthew 7:3.*

Even the sentence "You do the same things they do" does not reach the magnitude of the sin of those who presume to criticize and condemn others. Jesus said, "Why do you look at the speck in your brother's eye, but do not consider the plank in your own eye?"

His words describe those who are swift to discern defects in others. When they think they have detected a flaw in the character or the life, they are exceedingly zealous in trying to point it out. But Jesus declares that the very trait of character developed in doing this un-Christlike work is, in comparison with the fault criticized, as a beam in proportion to a dust mote. It is their own lack of the spirit of forbearance and love that leads them to make a world out of an atom. Those who have never experienced the contrition of an entire surrender to Christ do not in their life make manifest the softening influence of the Savior's love. They misrepresent the gentle, courteous spirit of the gospel and wound precious souls for whom Christ died. According to the imagery that our Savior uses, people who indulge a censorious spirit are guilty of greater sin than is the one they accuse, for they not only commit the same sin but add to it conceit and censoriousness.

Christ is the only true standard of character. Those who set themselves up as a standard for others are putting themselves in the place of Christ. Since the Father "has committed all judgment to the Son" (John 5:22), whoever presumes to judge the motives of others is again usurping the prerogative of the Son of God.

The sin that leads to the most unhappy results is the cold, critical, unforgiving spirit that characterizes Pharisaism. When the religious experience is devoid of love, Jesus is not there. No busy activity or Christless zeal can supply the lack. There may be a wonderful keenness of perception to discover the defects of others, but to everyone who indulges this spirit, Jesus says, "Hypocrite! First remove the plank from your own eye, and then you will see clearly to remove the speck from your brother's eye" (Matthew 7:5). Those who are guilty of wrong are the first to suspect wrong. By condemning another they are trying to conceal or excuse the evil of their own hearts. No sooner had Adam and Eve sinned than they began to accuse each other. This is what human nature will inevitably do when uncontrolled by the grace of Christ.

When people indulge this accusing spirit, they are not satisfied with pointing out what they suppose to be a defect in others. If milder means fail to make others do what they think ought to be done, they will resort to compulsion. Just as far as lies in their power they will force people to comply with their ideas of what is right. This is what the Jews did in the days of Christ and what the church has done ever since whenever it has lost the grace of Christ. Finding itself destitute of the power of love, it has reached out for the strong arm of the state to enforce its dogmas and execute its decrees.

Christ does not drive but draws men and women to Himself. The only compulsion which He employs is the constraint of love. When the church begins to seek the support of secular power, it is evident that it is devoid of the power of Christ—the constraint of divine love.

But the difficulty lies with the individual members of the church, and it is here that the cure must be wrought. Jesus bids accusers first to cast the beam out of their own eyes, renounce their censorious spirit, confess and forsake their own sins, before trying to correct others. For "a good tree does not bear bad fruit, nor does a bad tree bear good fruit" (Luke 6:43). This accusing spirit which you indulge is evil fruit, and shows that the tree is evil. What you need is a change of heart. You must have this experience before you are fitted to correct others.

When a crisis comes in the life of any soul, and you attempt to give counsel or admonition, your words will have only the weight of influence for good that your own example and spirit have gained for you. You must *be* good before you can *do* good. You cannot exert an influence that will transform others until your own heart has been humbled and refined and made tender by the grace of Christ. When this change has been wrought in you, it will be as natural for you to live to bless others as it is for the rosebush to yield its fragrant bloom or the grapevine its purple clusters.

If Christ is in you "the hope of glory" (Colossians 1:27), you will have no disposition to watch others, to expose their errors. Instead of seeking to accuse and condemn, it will be your object to help, to bless, and to save. In dealing with those who are in error, you will call to mind the many times you have erred and how hard it was to find the right way when you had once left it. You will not push brothers and sisters into greater darkness, but with a heart full of pity will tell them of their danger.

Those who look often upon the cross of Calvary, remembering that their sins placed the Savior there, will never try to estimate the degree of their guilt in comparison with that of others. They will not climb upon the judgment seat to bring accusation against another. There can be no spirit of criticism or self-exaltation on the part of those who walk in the shadow of Calvary's cross.

Not until you feel that you could sacrifice your own self-dignity, and even lay down your life in order to save an erring individual, have you cast the beam out of your own eye so that you are prepared to help others. Then you can approach them and touch their hearts. A tender spirit, a gentle, winning deportment, may save the erring and hide a multitude of sins. Let Christ be manifest through you, and He will reveal through you the creative energy of His word—a gentle yet mighty influence to re-create other souls in the beauty of the Lord our God.

"Do not give what is holy to the dogs." Matthew 7:6.

Jesus here refers to a class who have no desire to escape from the slavery of sin. By indulgence in the corrupt and vile their natures have become so degraded that they cling to the evil and will not be separated from it. The servants of Christ should not allow themselves to be hindered by those who would make the gospel only a matter of contention and ridicule.

But the Savior never passed by one soul, however sunken in sin, who was willing to receive the precious truths of heaven. To publicans and harlots His words were the beginning of a new life. Mary Magdalene, out of whom He cast seven devils, was the last at the Savior's tomb and the first whom He greeted on the morning of His resurrection. It was Saul of Tarsus, one of the most determined enemies of the gospel, who became Paul the devoted minister of Christ. Beneath an appearance of hatred and contempt, even beneath crime and degradation, may be hidden a soul that the grace of Christ will rescue to shine as a jewel in the Redeemer's crown.

"Ask, and it will be given to you; seek, and you will find; knock, and it will be opened to you." Matthew 7:7.

To leave no chance for unbelief, misunderstanding, or misinterpretation of His words, the Lord repeats the thrice-given promise. He longs to have those who would seek after God believe in Him who is able to do all things. Therefore He adds, "For everyone who asks receives, and he who seeks finds, and to him who knocks it will be opened" (verse 8).

The Lord specifies no conditions except that you hunger for His mercy, desire His counsel, and long for His love. "Ask." The asking makes it manifest that you realize your necessity. If you ask in faith you will receive. The Lord has pledged His word, and it cannot fail. If you come with true contrition, you need not feel that you are presumptuous in asking for what the Lord has promised. When you ask for the blessings you need, that you may perfect a character after Christ's likeness, the Lord assures you that you are asking according to a promise that will be verified. That you feel and know you are a sinner is sufficient ground for asking for His mercy and compassion. The condition upon which you may come to God is not that you shall be holy, but that you desire Him to cleanse you from all sin and purify you from all iniquity. The argument that we may plead now and ever is our great need, our utterly helpless state, that makes Him and His redeeming power a necessity.

"Search." Desire not merely His blessing, but Himself. Search, and you shall find. God is searching for you, and the very desire you feel to come to Him is but the drawing of His Spirit. Yield to that drawing. Christ is pleading the cause of the tempted, the erring, and the faithless. He is seeking to lift them into companionship with Himself. "If you seek Him, He will be found by you" (1 Chronicles 28:9).

"Knock." We come to God by special invitation, and He waits to welcome us to His audience chamber. The first disciples who followed Jesus were not satisfied with a hurried conversation with Him by the way. "They said, 'Rabbi . . . , where are You staying?' . . . They came and saw where He was staying, and remained with Him that day" (John 1:38, 39). So we may be admitted into closest communion with God. Let those who desire the blessing of God knock and wait at the door of mercy with firm assurance, saying, You, O Lord, have said that "everyone who asks receives, and he who seeks finds, and to him who knocks it will be opened."

Jesus looked upon those who were assembled to hear His words, and earnestly desired that the great multitude might appreciate the mercy and lovingkindness of God. As an illustration of their need, and of God's willingness to give, He presents before them a hungry child asking his earthly parent for bread. "What man is there among you," He said, "who, if his son asks for bread, will give him a stone?" (Matthew 7:9). He appeals to the tender, natural affection of parents for their children and then says, "If you then, being evil, know how to give good gifts to your children, how much more will your Father who is in heaven give good things to those who ask Him!" (verse 11). No man with a father's heart would turn from his son who is hungry and is asking for bread. Would he promise to give him good and nourishing food, and then give him a stone? And should anyone dishonor God by imagining that He would not respond to the appeals of His children?

"If you then, being evil, know how to give good gifts to your children, how much more will your heavenly Father give the Holy Spirit to those who ask Him!" (Luke 11:13). The Holy Spirit, the representative of Himself, is the greatest of all gifts. All "good gifts" are comprised in this. The Creator Himself can give us nothing greater, nothing better. When we beseech the Lord to pity us in our distress and to guide us by His Holy Spirit, He will never turn away our prayer. God can never reject the cry of the needy and longing heart. To those who in days of darkness feel that God is unmindful of them, this is the message from the Father's heart: "Can a woman forget her nursing child, and not have compassion on the son of her womb? Surely they may forget, yet I will not forget you. See, I have inscribed you on the palms of My hands" (Isaiah 49:15, 16).

Whatever spiritual blessing we need, it is our privilege to claim through Jesus.

Every promise in the Word of God furnishes us with subject matter for prayer, presenting the pledged word of Jehovah as our assurance. Whatever spiritual blessing we need, it is our privilege to claim through Jesus. We may tell the Lord, with the simplicity of a child, exactly what we need. We may state to Him our temporal matters, asking Him for bread and raiment as well as for the bread of life and the robe of Christ's righteousness. Your heavenly Father knows that you have need of all these things, and you are invited to ask Him concerning them. It is through the name of Jesus that every favor is received. God will honor that name and will supply your necessities from the riches of His liberality.

But do not forget that in coming to God as a father you acknowledge your relation to Him as a child. You not only trust His goodness but in all things yield to His will, knowing that His love is changeless. You give yourself to do His work. It was to those whom He had bidden to seek first the kingdom of God and His righteousness that Jesus gave the promise "Ask, and you will receive" (John 16:24).

Gifts that will satisfy the deepest craving of the heart, gifts that come through the costly sacrifice of the Redeemer's blood, gifts as lasting as eternity, will be received and enjoyed by all who will come to God as little children. Take God's promises as your own, plead them before Him as His own words, and you will receive fullness of joy.

"Whatever you want men to do to you, do also to them." Matthew 7:12.

On the assurance of the love of God toward us, Jesus enjoins love to one another, in one comprehensive principle covering all the relations of human fellowship. The standard of our obligation to others is found in what we ourselves would regard as their obligation to us.

In your association with others, put yourself in their place. Enter into their feelings, their difficulties, their disappointments, their joys, and their sorrows. Identify yourself with them, and then do to them as you would wish them to deal with you. This is another expression of the law, "You shall love your neighbor as yourself" (Matthew 22:39). It is a principle of heaven, and will be developed in all who are fitted for its holy companionship.

The golden rule is the principle of true courtesy, and its truest illustration is seen in the daily life of our Savior. What sweetness flowed from His very presence! The same spirit will be revealed in His children. Those with whom Christ dwells will be surrounded with a divine atmosphere. Their faces will reflect light from His, brightening the path for stumbling and weary feet.

No person who has the true ideal of what constitutes a perfect character will fail to manifest the sympathy and tenderness of Christ. The influence of grace is to soften the heart, to refine and purify the feelings, giving a heaven-born delicacy and sense of propriety.

But there is a yet deeper significance to the golden rule. All who have been made stewards of the manifold grace of God are called upon to impart to souls in ignorance and darkness, even as, were they in their place, they would desire them to impart to themselves. The apostle Paul said, "I am a debtor both to Greeks and to barbarians, both to wise and to unwise" (Romans 1:14). By all that you have known of the love of God, by all that you have received of the rich gifts of His grace above the most benighted and degraded souls upon the earth, are you in debt to those people to impart these gifts to them.

So also with the gifts and blessings of this life. Whatever you may possess above others places you in debt, to that degree, to all who are less favored. Have we wealth, or even the comforts of life, then we are under the most solemn obligation to care for the suffering sick, the widow, and the fatherless exactly as we would desire them to care for us were our condition and theirs to be reversed.

The golden rule teaches, by implication, the same truth which is taught elsewhere in the Sermon on the Mount, that "with the measure you use, it will be measured back to you" (Matthew 7:2). That which we do to others, whether it be good or evil, will surely react upon ourselves, in blessing or in cursing. Whatever we give, we shall receive again. The earthly blessings which we impart to others may be, and often are, repaid in kind. What we give does, in time of need, often come back to us in fourfold measure in the coin of the realm. But, besides this, all gifts are repaid, even in this life, in the fuller inflowing of God's love, which is the sum of all heaven's glory and its treasure. And evil imparted also returns again. All who have been free to condemn or discourage will in their own experience be brought over the ground where they have caused others to pass. They will feel what they have suffered because of their lack of sympathy and tenderness.

The standard of the golden rule is the true standard of Christianity. Anything short of it is a deception. A religion that leads people to place a low estimate upon human beings, whom Christ has esteemed of such value as to give Himself for them; a religion that would lead us to be careless of human needs, sufferings, or rights, is a spurious religion. It is because men and women take upon themselves the name of Christ, while in life they deny His character, that Christianity has so little power in the world.

Of the apostolic church, in those bright days when the glory of the risen Christ shone upon them, it is written that no believer said "that any of the things he possessed was his own" (Acts 4:32). "Nor was there anyone among them who lacked" (verse 34). "And with great power the apostles gave witness of the resurrection of the Lord Jesus. And great grace was upon them all" (verse 33).

When those who profess the name of Christ shall practice the principles of the golden rule, the same power will attend the gospel as in apostolic times.

"Narrow is the gate and difficult is the way which leads to life."
Matthew 7:14.

In the time of Christ the people of Palestine lived in walled towns, which were mostly situated upon hills or mountains. The gates, which were closed at sunset, were approached by steep, rocky roads. Travelers journeying homeward at the close of the day often had to press their way in eager haste up the difficult ascent in order to reach the gate before nightfall. The loiterer was left without.

The narrow, upward road leading to home and rest furnished Jesus with an impressive symbol of the Christian way. The path which I have set before you, He said, is narrow. The gate is difficult of entrance, for the golden rule excludes all pride and self-seeking. There is, indeed, a wider road, but its end is destruction. If you would climb the path of spiritual life, you must constantly ascend, for it is an upward way. You must go with the few, for the multitude will choose the downward path.

In the road to death the whole race may go, with all their worldliness, selfishness, pride, dishonesty, and moral abasement. There is room for everyone's opinions and doctrines, space to follow one's own inclinations, to do whatever self-love may dictate. As for the path that leads to destruction, there is no need to search for it. Its gate is wide, and the way is broad, and the feet naturally turn into the path that ends in death.

But the way to life is narrow and the entrance strait. If you cling to any besetting sin you will find the way too narrow for you to enter. Your own ways, your own will, your evil habits and practices, must be given up if you would keep the way of the Lord. Toil, patience, self-sacrifice, reproach, poverty, and the opposition of sinners was the portion of Christ, and it must be our portion, if we ever enter the Paradise of God.

Yet do not therefore conclude that the upward path is the hard way and the downward road the easy way. All along the road that leads to death there are pains and penalties, there are sorrows and disappointments, there are warnings not to go on. God's love has made it hard for the heedless and headstrong to destroy themselves. It is true that Satan's path is made to appear attractive, but it is all a deception. In the way of evil there are bitter remorse and cankering care. We may think it pleasant to follow pride and worldly ambition, but the end is pain and sorrow. Selfish plans may present flattering promises and hold out the hope of enjoyment, but we shall find that our happiness is poisoned and our life embittered by hopes that center in self.

"The way of the unfaithful is hard" (Proverbs 13:15), but wisdom's ways "are ways of pleasantness, and all her paths are peace" (Proverbs 3:17). Every act of obedience to Christ, every act of self-denial for His sake, every trial well endured, every victory gained over temptation, is a step in the march to the glory of final victory. If we take Christ for our guide, He will lead us safely. Though the path is so narrow, so holy that sin cannot be tolerated therein, yet access has been secured for all, and not one doubting, trembling soul need say, "God cares nothing for me."

Those who walk in wisdom's ways are, even in tribulation, exceeding joyful, for He whom their soul loves walks, invisible, beside them.

The road may be rough and the ascent steep, with pitfalls upon the right hand and upon the left. We may have to endure toil in our journey; when faint, we may have to fight; when discouraged, we must still hope. But with Christ as our guide we shall not fail of reaching the desired haven at last.

And all the way up the steep road leading to eternal life are well-springs of joy to refresh the weary. Those who walk in wisdom's ways are, even in tribulation, exceeding joyful, for He whom their soul loves walks, invisible, beside them. At each upward step they discern more distinctly the touch of His hand. At every step brighter gleamings of glory from the Unseen fall upon their path. Their songs of praise, reaching ever a higher note, ascend to join the songs of angels before the throne.

"Strive to enter through the narrow gate." Luke 13:24.

Belated travelers, hurrying to reach the city gate before dark, could not turn aside for any attractions along the way. Their whole mind was bent on the one purpose of entering the gate. The same intensity of purpose, said Jesus, is required in the Christian life. I have opened to you the glory of character, which is the true glory of My kingdom. It offers you no promise of earthly dominion, yet it is worthy of your supreme desire and effort. I do not call you to battle for the supremacy of the world's great empire, but do not therefore conclude that there is no battle to be fought nor victories to be won. I bid you strive, agonize, to enter into My spiritual kingdom.

The Christian life is a battle and a march. But the victory to be gained is not won by human power. The field of conflict is the domain of the heart. The battle which we have to fight is the surrender of self to the will of God, the yielding of the heart to the sovereignty of love. The old nature, born of blood and of the will of the flesh, cannot inherit the kingdom of God. The hereditary tendencies, the former habits, must be given up.

Those who determine to enter the spiritual kingdom will find that all the powers and passions of an unregenerate nature, backed by the forces of the kingdom of darkness, are arrayed against them. Selfishness and pride will make a stand against anything that would show them to be sinful. We cannot, of ourselves, conquer the evil desires and habits that strive for the mastery. God alone can give us the victory. He desires us to have the mastery over ourselves, our own will and ways. But He cannot work in us without our consent and cooperation. The divine Spirit works through our faculties and powers. Our energies are required to cooperate with God.

The victory is not won without much earnest prayer, without the humbling of self at every step. Our will is not to be forced into cooperation with divine agencies, but it must be voluntarily submitted. Were it possible to force upon you with a hundredfold greater intensity the influence of the Spirit of God, it would not make you a Christian, a fit subject for heaven. The stronghold of Satan would not be broken. The will must be placed on the side of God's will. You are not able, of yourself, to bring your purposes and desires and inclinations into submission to the will of God. But if you are "willing to be made willing," God will accomplish the work for you, "bringing every thought into captivity to the obedience of Christ" (2 Corinthians 10:5). Then you will "work out your own salvation with fear and trembling; for it is God who works in you both to will and to do for His good pleasure" (Philippians 2:12, 13).

But many, while attracted by the beauty of Christ and the glory of heaven, yet shrink from the conditions by which alone these can become their own. Many in the broad way are not fully satisfied with the path in which they walk. They long to break from the slavery of sin, and in their own strength they seek to make a stand against their sinful practices. But selfish pleasure, love of the world, pride, unsanctified ambition, place a barrier between them and the Savior. To renounce their own will, their chosen objects of affection or pursuit, requires a sacrifice at which they hesitate and falter and turn back. "Many . . . will seek to enter and will not be able" (Luke 13:24). They desire the good and make some effort to obtain it, but they do not have a settled purpose to secure it at the cost of all things.

The only hope for us if we would overcome is to unite our will to God's will and work in cooperation with Him, hour by hour and day by day. We cannot retain self and yet enter the kingdom of God. If we ever attain unto holiness, it will be through the renunciation of self and the reception of the mind of Christ. Pride and self-sufficiency must be crucified. Are we willing to pay the price required of us? Are we willing to have our will brought into perfect conformity to the will of God? Until we are willing, the transforming grace of God cannot be manifest upon us.

Jacob, in the great crisis of his life, turned aside to pray. He was filled with one overmastering purpose—to seek for transformation of character. But while he was pleading with God, an enemy, as he supposed, placed his hand upon him, and all night he wrestled for his life. But the purpose of his soul was not changed by peril of life itself. When his strength was nearly spent, the Angel put forth His divine power, and at His touch Jacob knew Him with whom he had been struggling. Wounded and helpless, he fell upon the Savior's breast, pleading for a blessing. He would not be turned aside nor cease his intercession. Jacob pleaded with determined spirit, "I will not let You go unless You bless me!" (Genesis 32:26).

This spirit of persistence was inspired by Him who wrestled with the patriarch. It was He who gave him the victory, and He changed his name from Jacob to Israel, saying, "You have struggled with God and with men, and have prevailed" (verse 28). That for which Jacob had vainly wrestled in his own strength was won through self-surrender and steadfast faith. "This is the victory that has overcome the world—our faith" (1 John 5:4).

Teachers of falsehood will arise to draw you away from the narrow path and the strait gate. Beware of them. Though concealed in sheep's clothing, inwardly they are ravening wolves. Jesus gives a test by which false teachers may be distinguished from the true. "You will know them by their fruits," He says. "Do men gather grapes from thornbushes or figs from thistles?" (verse 16).

We are not bidden to prove them by their fair speeches and exalted professions. They are to be judged by the Word of God. "To the law and to the testimony! If they do not speak according to this word, it is because there is no light in them" (Isaiah 8:20). What message do these teachers bring? Does it lead you to reverence and fear God? Does it lead you to manifest your love for Him by loyalty to His commandments? If people do not feel the weight of the moral law; if they make light of God's precepts; if they break one of the least of His commandments and teach others to do so, they shall be of no esteem in the sight of heaven. We may know that their claims are without foundation. They are doing the very work that originated with the prince of darkness, the enemy of God.

> *When benevolence, kindness, tenderheartedness, sympathy, are manifest in our lives; when the joy of right doing is in our hearts; when we exalt Christ, and not self, we may know that our faith is of the right order.*

Not all who profess His name and wear His badge are Christ's. Many who have taught in My name, said Jesus, will be found wanting at last. "Many will say to Me in that day, 'Lord, Lord, have we not prophesied in Your name, cast out demons in Your name, and done many wonders in Your name?' And then I will declare to them, 'I never knew you; depart from Me, you who practice lawlessness'" (Matthew 7:22, 23).

There are persons who believe that they are right, when they are wrong. While claiming Christ as their Lord, and professedly doing great works in His name, they work iniquity. "With their mouth they show much love me, but their hearts desire their own gain" (Ezekiel 33:31). Those who declare God's Word are to them "as a very lovely song of one who has a pleasant voice and can play well on an instrument; for they hear your words, but they do not do them" (verse 32).

A mere profession of discipleship is of no value. The faith in Christ which saves the soul is not what it is represented to be by many. "Believe, believe," they say, "and you need not keep the law." But a belief that does not lead to obedience is presumption. The apostle John says, "He who says, 'I know Him,' and does not keep His commandments, is a liar, and the truth is not in him" (1 John 2:4). Let none cherish the idea that special providences or miraculous manifestations are to be the proof of the genuineness of their work or of the ideas they advocate. When persons will speak lightly of the Word of God, and set their impressions, feelings, and exercises above the divine standard, we may know that they have no light in them.

Obedience is the test of discipleship. It is the keeping of the commandments that proves the sincerity of our professions of love. When the doctrine we accept kills sin in the heart, purifies the soul from defilement, bears the fruit of holiness, we may know that it is the truth of God. When benevolence, kindness, tenderheartedness, sympathy, are manifest in our lives; when the joy of right doing is in our hearts; when we exalt Christ, and not self, we may know that our faith is of the right order. "Now by this we know that we know Him, if we keep His commandments" (verse 3).

"It did not fall, for it was founded on the rock." Matthew 7:25.

The people had been deeply moved by the words of Christ. The divine beauty of the principles of truth attracted them. Christ's solemn warnings had come to them as the voice of the heart-searching God. His words had struck at the very root of their former ideas and opinions. To obey His teaching would require a change in all their habits of thought and action. It would bring them into collision with their religious teachers, for it would involve the overthrow of the whole structure which for generations the rabbis had been rearing. Therefore, while the hearts of the people responded to His words, few were ready to accept them as the guide of life.

Jesus ended His teaching on the mount with an illustration that presented with startling vividness the importance of putting in practice the words He had spoken. Among the crowds that thronged about the Savior were many who had spent their lives about the Sea of Galilee. As they sat upon the hillside, listening to the words of Christ, they could see valleys and ravines through which the mountain streams found their way to the sea. In summer these streams often wholly disappeared, leaving only a dry and dusty channel. But when the wintry storms burst upon the hills, fierce, raging torrents filled the channels, at times overspreading the valleys and bearing everything away on their resistless flood. Often, then, the hovels reared by the peasants on the grassy plain, apparently beyond the reach of danger, were swept away. But high upon the hills were houses built upon the rock. In some parts of the land were dwellings built wholly of rock, and many of them had withstood the tempests of a thousand years. These houses were reared with toil and difficulty. Their location appeared less inviting than the grassy plain. But they were founded upon the rock, and wind and flood and tempest beat upon them in vain.

Like the builders of these houses on the rock, said Jesus, are those who shall receive the words that I have spoken to you, and make them the foundation of their character and life. Centuries before, the prophet Isaiah had written, "The word of our God stands forever" (Isaiah 40:8). Peter, long after the Sermon on the Mount was given, quoted these words of Isaiah and then added, "This is the word which by the gospel was preached to you" (1 Peter 1:25). The Word of God is the only steadfast thing our world knows. It is the sure foundation. "Heaven and earth will pass away," said Jesus, "but My words will by no means pass away" (Matthew 24:35).

The great principles of the law, of the very nature of God, are embodied in the words of Christ on the mount. Whoever builds upon them is building upon Christ, the Rock of Ages. In receiving the Word, we receive Christ. And only those who thus receive His words are building upon Him. "For no other foundation can anyone lay than that which is laid, which is Jesus Christ" (1 Corinthians 3:11). "There is no other name under heaven given among men by which we must be saved" (Acts 4:12). Christ, the Word, the revelation of God—the manifestation of His character, His law, His love, His life—is the only foundation upon which we can build a character that will endure.

We build on Christ by obeying His Word. It is not those who merely enjoy righteousness that are righteous, but those who do righteousness. Holiness is the result of surrendering all to God. It is doing the will of our heavenly Father. When the children of Israel camped on the borders of the Promised Land, it was not enough for them to have a knowledge of Canaan or to sing the songs of Canaan. This alone would not bring them into possession of its vineyards and olive groves. They could make it theirs in truth only by occupation, by complying with the conditions, by exercising living faith in God, by appropriating His promises to themselves, while they obeyed His instruction.

Religion consists in doing the words of Christ—not to earn God's favor, but because, all undeserving, we have received the gift of His love. Christ places the salvation of human beings not upon profession merely, but upon faith made manifest in works of righteousness. Doing, not saying merely, is expected of the followers of Christ. It is through action that character is built. "As many as are *led* by the Spirit of God, these are the sons of God" (Romans 8:14). Not those whose hearts are touched by the Spirit, not those who now and then yield to its power, but they that are led by the Spirit, are the children of God.

*D*o you desire to become a follower of Christ, yet know not how to begin? Are you in darkness and know not how to find the light? Follow the light you have. Set your heart to obey what you do know of the Word of God. His power—His very life— dwells in His Word. As you receive the word in faith, it will give you power to obey. As you heed the light you have, greater light will come. You are building on God's Word, and your character will be built after the character of Christ.

Christ, the true foundation, is a living stone. His life is imparted to all that are built upon Him. "You also, as living stones, are being built up a spiritual house" (1 Peter 2:5). "The whole building, being fitted together, grows into a holy temple in the Lord" (Ephesians 2:21). The stones became one with the foundation. That building no tempest can overthrow.

But every building erected on any other foundation than God's Word will fall. Those who build on the foundation of human ideas and opinions, of forms and human ceremonies, or on any works independent of the grace of Christ are erecting the structure of character upon shifting sand. The fierce tempests of temptation will sweep away the sandy foundation and leave their house a wreck on the shores of time.

But today mercy pleads with the sinner. The voice that speaks to the impenitent today is the voice of Him who in anguish exclaimed as He beheld the city of His love: "O Jerusalem, Jerusalem, the one who kills the prophets and stones those who are sent to her! How often I wanted to gather your children together, as a hen gathers her brood under her wings, but you were not willing! See! Your house is left to you desolate" (Luke 13:34, 35).

In Jerusalem, Jesus beheld a symbol of the world that had despised and rejected His grace. He was weeping, O stubborn heart, for you! Even when Jesus' tears were shed upon the mount, Jerusalem might yet have repented and escaped its doom. For a little space the Gift of heaven still waited its acceptance. So to you Christ is still speaking in accents of love: "Behold, I stand at the door and knock. If anyone hears My voice and opens the door, I will come in to him and dine with him, and he with Me" (Revelation 3:20). "Behold, now is the accepted time; behold, now is the day of salvation" (2 Corinthians 6:2).

You who are resting your hope on self are building on the sand. But it is not yet too late to escape the impending ruin. Before the tempest breaks, flee to the sure foundation. "Behold, I lay in Zion a stone for a foundation, a tried stone, a precious cornerstone, a sure foundation" (Isaiah 28:16). "Look to Me, and be saved, all you ends of the earth! For I am God, and there is no other" (Isaiah 45:22). "Fear not, for I am with you; be not dismayed, for I am your God. I will strengthen you, yes, I will help you. I will uphold you with My righteous right hand" (Isaiah 41:10).